Praise for *Bre*

"Alan Jacobs's *Breaking Bre* .... one's reading list in these times of what a friend of mine calls 'disagreement phobia' on all sides in politics and life. Jacobs thoughtfully discusses the benefits of reading long-dead authors—even though Edith Wharton was an anti-Semite and David Hume a racist. In this way we practice encountering minds different, and sometimes objectionable, to our own, and find the good, useful, and beautiful admixed with the difficult and repulsive. Right and left, young and old, we need this skill more than ever now."

—Naomi Alderman, *The Spectator* (London)

"Jacobs is a proponent of difference and distance as a means of increasing perspective. . . . When we pick up an old book, we know that 'another human being from another world has spoken to us.' That sense of appreciation may well be applied to the work of all writers, living and dead. There are many worlds, past and present, from which another may speak." —John Glassie, *The Washington Post*

"Brave . . . Jacobs, who has taught college-level literature courses for many years, has clearly honed his thoughts in the classroom. He questions the knee-jerk tendency to reject anyone or anything that does not fully accord with a preferred social or political view. . . . There are moments of great insight here." —Wendy Lesser, *The New York Times*

"*Breaking Bread with the Dead* is concerned with the challenge, and personal benefit, of connecting with authors far from our own experience. . . . Through a combination of examples and theoretical exposition, Jacobs argues that by engaging responsibly with long-gone authors, we allow their voices to teach us. . . . Jacobs is especially aware of the challenge of texts that don't match our prejudices: We need not demonize them, nor relinquish our convictions, but should simply work to seek community with past thinkers. Our 'personal density' is a matter of experiencing shared membership, across time and place, with other parts of humanity."

—Joshua P. Hochschild, *First Things*

"Jacobs marshals an impressive body of evidence from writers as diverse as Horace and Zadie Smith to craft his argument for sympathetic engagement with sources whose ideas may seem strange, or

even repulsive. . . . At a time when many Americans, compelled by tragic events to confront a legacy of racism, are engaged in deep reflection about the meaning of the nation's history, [this] is an exceptionally useful companion for those who want to do so with honesty and integrity."
—*Shelf Awareness*

"The ideas are stimulating. . . . Will give thoughtful readers a jumping-off point for further reflection."
—*Publishers Weekly*

"Alan Jacobs has given us a toolbox stocked with concepts that balance the pop of a self-help book with the depth of a college seminar. *Breaking Bread with the Dead* is an invitation, but even more than that, an emancipation: from the buzzing prison of the here and now into the wide-open field of the past."
—Robin Sloan, author of *Sourdough*

"A provocative self-help book that challenges conventional wisdom about why we read and where it can bring us. We are distracted, and today our reading, from link to link, has left us light. We need engagement and, most of all, we need the grounding and weight from knowing our past. This elegant book moved me, especially when it led me to rethink time with my mentors and how they taught me, to paraphrase Wordsworth, what to love and how to love. On so many pages I found things I know I will carry forward."
—Sherry Turkle, Professor of Social Studies of Science and Technology at MIT, bestselling author of *Reclaiming Conversation* and *Alone Together*

"Alan Jacobs captures the nervous joy of helping students discover that writers of 'the long ago and far away' can mitigate the feeling of unmoored loneliness that afflicts so many young people today. Never scolding or didactic, *Breaking Bread with the Dead* is a compassionate book about the saving power of reading and a moving account of how writers of the past can help us cope in the frantic present."
—Andrew Delbanco, author of *The War Before the War*

"A beautiful case for reading old books as a way to cultivate personal depth in shallow times. *Breaking Bread with the Dead* is timely and timeless—the perfect ending to the trilogy Alan Jacobs began with *The Pleasures of Reading in an Age of Distraction* and continued with *How to Think*. I've stolen so much from these books. So will you."
—Austin Kleon, bestselling author of *Steal Like an Artist*

PENGUIN BOOKS

BREAKING BREAD WITH THE DEAD

Alan Jacobs is Distinguished Professor of Humanities in the Honors Program at Baylor University. He has published fifteen books and writes for publications such as *The Atlantic*, *Harper's Magazine*, *The Christian Century*, *The New Yorker*, and *The Wall Street Journal*.

ALSO BY ALAN JACOBS

The Year of Our Lord 1943:
Christian Humanism in an Age of Crisis

How to Think:
A Survival Guide for a World at Odds

The Book of Common Prayer:
A Biography

The Pleasures of Reading in an Age of Distraction

Wayfaring:
Essays Pleasant and Unpleasant

Original Sin:
A Cultural History

The Narnian:
The Life and Imagination of C. S. Lewis

BREAKING BREAD

with

THE DEAD

*A Reader's Guide to a More
Tranquil Mind*

A<small>LAN</small> J<small>ACOBS</small>

PENGUIN BOOKS

PENGUIN BOOKS
An imprint of Penguin Random House LLC
penguinrandomhouse.com

First published in the United States of America by Penguin Press,
an imprint of Penguin Random House LLC, 2020
Published in Penguin Books 2021

ISBN 9781984878427 (paperback)

THE LIBRARY OF CONGRESS HAS CATALOGED THE HARDCOVER EDITION AS FOLLOWS:
Names: Jacobs, Alan, 1958– author.
Title: Breaking bread with the dead:
a reader's guide to a more tranquil mind / Alan Jacobs.
Description: New York: Penguin Press, 2020. |
Includes bibliographical references and index.
Identifiers: LCCN 2020000756 (print) | LCCN 2020000757 (ebook) |
ISBN 9781984878403 (hardcover) | ISBN 9781984878410 (ebook)
Subjects: LCSH: Literature and society. | Social problems in literature. |
Anxiety in literature. | Presentism (Philosophy)
Classification: LCC PN51 .J255 2020 (print) |
LCC PN51 (ebook) | DDC 809—dc23
LC record available at https://lccn.loc.gov/2020000756
LC ebook record available at https://lccn.loc.gov/2020000757

Printed in the United States of America

Designed by Amanda Dewey

CONTENTS

PREFACE

I've been a teacher for many years now, and one of the best things about teaching is the way it presses you to revisit decisions you made in decades past, to defend and explain actions that for you long ago ceased to need defense or explanation. What you find precious strikes some, or all, of your students as wholly without value; and they want to discuss matters in class that if you had your way you'd never consider again. Nevertheless, there you all are, stuck in the same room together several hours a week, for a dozen or more weeks.

It's possible, of course, if you're the teacher anyway, simply to ignore the problem and do Your Thing as you define Your Thing. In this context I think often of one of *my* former teachers, who commented that he had taught a particular course for so many years, and taught it in precisely the same way, that he often had a sensation, when he was in the middle of a lecture he knew by rote, that he could stroll right out of the classroom and his voice would simply continue droning its familiar drone until the appointed words were all said.

I vowed when I first heard this story that I would some-how avoid this dreadful fate, and that vow commits me to noticing when my students are and are not paying atten-tion, when they're puzzled, when they're annoyed, when they're bored. It commits me to answering them as faith-fully as I can when they wonder (either openly or covertly) why we do what we do, read what we read, ask what we ask. And I am very glad that I made that vow, because it has prevented me from settling prematurely on easy and facile accounts of my calling as a teacher.

Among the fruits of that vow has been a series of books, of which this is the third, that attempt to communicate to the general reader much of what I have learned over the years by taking my students' questions and boredom seri-ously. The first is called *The Pleasures of Reading in an Age of Distraction*, and the second is called *How to Think*, and now here we are discussing the value of paying attention to old books that come from strange times and are written in peculiar language and frankly don't make a whole lot of sense. Much of what I have to say here is what I have tried to convey to my students, though rarely in terms as explicit as I lay out here. Maybe some of my former students will read this book and think, *Oh,* that's *what he was up to.*

I write here not as a teacher to students but rather as a reader to other readers, a citizen to other citizens. I write because I think I have learned a few things in my teaching life that are relevant to our common life. You will see what those are if you read on.

My approach here is anything but systematic. Of all the literary genres, I am fondest of the essay, with its meandering course that (we hope) faithfully represents the meanderings of the human mind. Like the poet Yeats, I often find that thought, and indeed life as a whole, is like a winding stair: you keep revisiting the same points, the same themes, but at higher levels of experience. From those ascending vantage points a given idea, a given feeling, a given perception, is recognizably itself and yet somehow different. One's understanding of it becomes richer, sometimes in ways that are continuous, sometimes in ways that are revolutionary. I have tried to mimic that spiraling ascent in the pages that follow. A theme or notion is introduced, considered, dropped—and then picked up again later in light of additional readings, further reflections. Certain images and events and people will recur throughout this book, returning perhaps when you think we're done with them. I write this way because none of the things I care about most have ever proven susceptible to systematic exposition.

INTRODUCTION

Sometimes I teach old books to young people, and recently I was teaching the *Epistles* of the Roman poet
Horace to a group of undergraduates. For many centuries
there were few authors more widely read than Horace,
though to be fair most of the readers were boys forced to
translate him from Latin when they would far rather have
been playing some kind of ball game. Some old dude sitting
in a farmhouse writing rhythmical letters to friends—this
was not exactly a recipe for delight.

Maybe my students—mostly young women, these
days—also thought they had better things to do. But then
we got to one of the *Epistles*, addressed to one Lollius Maximus, in which Horace wonders how one might acquire "a
tranquil mind."

A tranquil mind. Who doesn't need that?

Often at the beginning of a class I will give my students a brief reading quiz—unannounced in advance; yes,
I'm *that* kind of teacher—which has the salutary effect of
making sure that everyone is in class on time. The room is

always full when I walk in, and fairly regularly the first thing I see is every head bowed before a glowing screen. Sometimes they don't even look up when I say hello. Often their brows are furrowed; they may look anxious or worried. They dutifully put their phones away as soon as class begins, whether it does so with a quiz or a question, but during the discussion I occasionally see hands twitch or reach toward bags. If I see phones left on the seminar-room table I lightly (but seriously) suggest that they be put away to minimize temptation. All my students have mastered the art of packing up their bags at the end of class with one hand while checking messages with the other. They leave the room with heads once more down, and brows once more furrowed, navigating like a blind person through her familiar living room.

I know how they feel. When my students are taking a quiz there's nothing for me to do, so *my* hand then drifts toward my phone—or did, until I finally forced myself to stop carrying my phone around; and my twitchiness during quizzes was among the chief factors that pushed me to that decision. That twitchiness—that constant low-level anxiety at being communicatively unstimulated—seems so normal now that we may be slightly disconcerted when it's absent. That's why a tweet by Jason Gay, a writer for *The Wall Street Journal*, went viral a few years ago: "There's a guy in this coffee shop sitting at a table, not on his phone, not on a laptop, just drinking coffee, like a psychopath." A man not justifying his existence through constant work or constant social connectivity? Psychopathy seems the only logical explanation. Unless, of course, he happens to possess a tranquil mind.

The old man in an Italian farmhouse, two thousand years ago, thought a lot about how you might acquire such a mind. "What brings tranquility?" he asks his friend Lollius Maximus, or rather muses *to* Lollius. "What makes you care less?"

What did Horace need to "care less" *about*? It's worth taking a moment to tell his story. His father had probably been born a slave; certainly he had spent some time in slavery. Eventually he was able to purchase his freedom and made a career that allowed him to offer his gifted son (born 65 BCE) the best education on offer, including a period at the great Academy in Athens that had been founded by Plato. Later Horace was both a soldier—a very bad one, he said—and a political activist, though unfortunately for him he was active in opposition to Octavian, who would become Augustus Caesar. He had his property confiscated and fell into poverty; he began writing poetry; his poetry came to the attention of a powerful politician and ally of Octavian named Maecenas; Maecenas became Horace's patron and bought him a farm in the Sabine countryside.

And that's how he came to sit in a farmhouse to contemplate just what it is that gives you a tranquil mind. He had been plucked from the complex and overlapping dangers of a politically engaged person in Rome during a period of intermittent civil war, and set down in the peaceful countryside. And yet his mind continually twitched toward that mad world he had fled from; because, after all, all roads lead to Rome. Rome is where the action is: the festive dinners that collapsed into political argument, the drinking parties that served as cover for conspiracy, the fortuitous encounters in the streets that led to the whispered exchange of gossip. . . . You were always in danger in Rome; but you were always *connected*. In the country nothing happened—unless it happened in your mind.

Horace thinks and thinks and thinks about these things, and writes his letters that are also poems to far-flung friends—letters, therefore, that are also meant for strangers. And so we strangers to Horace and strangers to Rome, fifteen people sitting in an air-conditioned room in central Texas, a place Horace could never have imagined, sat with his poems before us and realized that we wanted to know exactly what Horace wanted to know, and for many of the same reasons. We wanted tranquil minds. We wanted to escape our addiction to the adrenaline rush of connectivity.

When Horace advises Lollius Maximus he also advises himself—indeed, the poem may do the latter more than the former. "Interrogate the writings of the wise," he counsels.

Asking them to tell you how you can
Get through your life in a peaceable tranquil way.
Will it be greed, that always feels poverty-stricken,
That harasses and torments you all your days?
Will it be hope and fear about trivial things,
In anxious alternation in your mind?
Where is it virtue comes from, is it from books?
Or is it a gift from Nature that can't be learned?
What is the way to become a friend to yourself?
What brings tranquility? What makes you care less?

(I am using David Ferry's marvelous translation.) Horace exhorts himself, and us, to "interrogate the writings of the wise"—the sorts of thinkers, perhaps, that he studied when he was at the Academy in Athens—because they *are* wise, of course, but for another reason as well: they are *alien* to us, they are not part of our habitual round. They draw us out of our daily, our endlessly cyclical, obsessions with money and with "trivial things"—the kinds of obsessions that "harass" us, that "torment" us, that make us jump from thought to thought, or rather emotion to emotion, in "anxious alternation."

It's useful to see that these anxieties have plagued people who lived so long ago, even if we feel them with particular intensity today—as we probably do. One of the consequences of an individualist society such as ours, a society in which each of us is expected to forge her own identity according to her own lights, is that we feel what the sociologist Norbert Elias called "pressure for foresight," the compulsion (perhaps a better translation of Elias's German) to look ahead into a future for which we must plan, but which—the future being *the future*—we cannot see. That is why some therapists who work with young people today say that the single greatest source of stress and anxiety for them is the sheer number of *choices* they have before them, which generates the fear that if they make the wrong choices they may not be able to overcome their own errors. And my long experience as a teacher confirms this interpretation.

Horace exhorts Lollius, exhorts himself, exhorts *us*, to shift our attention from those compulsions toward questions that really and always matter—"Where is it virtue comes from?"—because even by just exploring those questions, even if we fail to answer them, we're pushing back against the tyranny of everyday anxieties. We're resisting, or evading, the stresses that a condition of always-on connectivity inevitably brings to us, in large part because when we are so connected we are constantly driven to compare ourselves to others who have made better choices than we have. (Or so we think, forgetting that Instagram is a great deceiver in these matters.)

You can tell that Horace was a convivial sort. Living a life of simple silent contemplation ("like a psychopath") wasn't for him. But he knew also that the life of politically obsessed Rome was dangerous to him in more ways than one. Even when he wasn't in danger of being imprisoned or killed for being a rebel, he was in danger of having his mind colonized by anxieties large and small. He therefore sought to receive his Sabine farm as a refuge, as a place where he could walk down by the tree-shaded brook, and enjoy the local wine; where he could return to his house and write long intricate letters to friends; where he could "interrogate the writings of the wise." The *past* became a companion to him in what otherwise might have felt an exile, because, as L. P. Hartley famously says at the outset of his novel *The Go-Between*, "The past is a foreign country; they do things differently there." Which of course doesn't mean that what "they do" is always right—but awareness of it is always illuminating, and often liberating.

We sat in our Texas classroom and thought about this. Horace reached out from long ago and far away to tell us that we should ourselves reach out to the long ago and far away. He was not like us; and yet he spoke to us health-giving words. That he was not like us—that he spoke from a world whose contours made it so different from ours—made those words somehow easier to receive.

My students and I were reflecting on the current of our own daily lives, which is not an insignificant thing to think about; but the past can touch us and teach us unexpectedly in matters of broader import. In 2016, the Indian novelist Amitav Ghosh published a nonfiction book called *The Great Derangement: Climate Change and the Unthinkable*. One of the themes of the book is the relative absence of climate change in contemporary fiction: it is strange, Ghosh thought, that our storytellers could be so silent about events that are so enormously consequential for the entire planet. And as he tried to write his own novel confronting climate change, he found few resources to help him among his fellow writers today. Yes, there is a small subgenre of climate fiction, "cli-fi," as it is sometimes called; but it tends to look predictively or dystopically toward the future. How do we reckon with the experience of *now*?

Ghosh told the journalist Wen Stephenson about a realization that, as he asked that question, came to him: "You know, after I finished writing *The Great Derangement*, I felt that to look to late-twentieth-century literature for any form of response to what we are facing today is useless. It offers no resources. It's so much centered on the individual, so much centered on identity, it really doesn't give us any way of thinking about these issues." So what, then, to do, if you're a writer who is craving some kind of model or example for creative engagement with such massive forces? "I decided that . . . I must go back and read *pre-modern literature*. And I'm fortunate that I can read pre-modern Bengali literature." And as he started reading these old, old tales from his own cultural past, he was surprised: "So I started reading these stories, and you know, it's really remarkable how aware they are, how responsive they are to catastrophe, disaster, to the stuff that's happening around them, even though it's not at all in a realist vein. But it's there. It's omnipresent." It was from his ancestors, not from his contemporaries, that he learned how to think about the experience of living through environmental changes so massive that they dwarf human imagination.

Ghosh concluded that reading works from the past "really teaches you that what has happened, what modernity has done is, literally, made this work of recognition impossible." That is, modern consciousness has taken certain forms that don't just *ignore* the experiences that he wants to write about but *disable* us from understanding them. But modern consciousness is not all we have to draw upon.

To read old books is to get an education in possibility for next to nothing. Watching the latest social-media war break out, I often recall Grace Kelly's character in *High Noon*, a Quaker pacifist, saying, "I don't care who's right or who's wrong. There's got to be some better way for people to live." (That by the end of the movie she abandons her pacifism only, if ironically, emphasizes the importance of her point.) The suspicion that there's got to be some better way for people to live has the salutary effect of suppressing reflex. To open yourself to the past is to make yourself less vulnerable to the cruelties of descending in tweeted wrath on a young woman whose clothing you disapprove of, or firing an employee because of a tweet you didn't take time to understand, or responding to climate change either by ignoring it or by indulging in impotent rage. You realize that you need not obey the impulses of this moment—which, it is fair to say, never tend to produce a tranquil mind.

1.

PRESENTISM AND
TEMPORAL BANDWIDTH

ear the beginning of Martin Rowson's graphic adap-
tation of *The Communist Manifesto*, there's a picture of
a big sign reading, as does the sign over the gates of Hell in
Dante's *Inferno*, LASCIATE OGNE SPERANZA VOI CH'INTRATE—
"Abandon all hope, ye who enter here." Rowson has that
sign fronting an edifice labeled "All History Hitherto."*
That neatly sums up a common current attitude: all history
hitherto is at best a sewer of racism, sexism, homophobia,
and general social injustice, at worst an abattoir which no
reasonable person would even want to peek at.

It's not hard to spot the trend: a writer tells us to stop
reading *Robinson Crusoe* because it's a document of racist,
sexist colonialism; a librarian grieves at the space books
by dead white men occupy on the shelves of her library; a

---

*He gets the "All History Hitherto" line from the first sentence of the first chapter of
The Communist Manifesto (1848) by Marx and Engels: "The history of all hitherto existing
society is the history of class struggles."

professor of architecture rejoices at the "liberation" offered by the burning of Notre-Dame de Paris; a reader can't bear to be in the very presence of a classic novel featuring a vivid streak of anti-Semitism ("I don't want anyone like that in my house").

There is an increasing sense not just that the past is sadly in error, is superannuated and irrelevant and full of foul ideas that we're well rid of, but that it actually *defiles* us—its presence makes us unclean.

This business of defilement is both interesting in itself and important for the story I have to tell. I'm going to argue here that the sense of defilement is to a great degree evoked first by *information overload*—a sense that we are always receiving more sheer data than we know how to evaluate—and a more general feeling of *social acceleration*—the perception that the world is not only changing but changing faster and faster. What those closely related experiences tend to require from us is a rough-and-ready kind of *informational triage*.

Triage—it's a French word meaning to separate and sort—is what nurses and doctors on the battlefield do: during and after a battle, as wounded soldiers flow in, the limited resources of a medical unit are sorely tested. The medical staff must learn to make instantaneous judgments: this person needs treatment *now*, that one can wait a little while, a third one will have to wait longer, preferably somewhere other than the medical tent. To the wounded soldiers, this system will often seem peremptory and harsh, uncompassionate, and perhaps even cruel; but it's absolutely necessary for the nurses and doctors to be ruthlessly brisk. They cannot afford for one soldier to die while they're comforting one whose injuries don't threaten his life.

Navigating daily life in the internet age is a lot like doing battlefield triage. Given that what cultural critic Matthew Crawford calls the "attentional commons" is constantly noisy—there are days we can't even put gas in our cars without being assaulted by advertisements blared at ear-rattling volume—we also learn to be ruthless in deciding how to deploy our attention. We only have so much of it, and often the decision of whether or not to "pay" it must be made in an instant. To avoid madness we must learn to reject appeals to our time, and reject them without hesitation or pity.

But to this problem of informational overload we have to add another: what the sociologist Hartmut Rosa calls "social acceleration." It's a familiar experience. People were starting to feel that the social pedal was thrust to the metal even fifty years ago. Consider, as an example, "Slow Tuesday Night," a story by the American science fiction writer R. A. Lafferty. Lafferty imagines that some future researchers will discover the "Abebaios block," a feature of our brains that slows down our decision making.* Once the block is removed our mentation accelerates, as do our social connections. So Lafferty begins his story by describing a panhandler who proposes marriage to "Ildefonsa Impala, the most beautiful woman in the city":

Abebaios is a Greek word meaning fickle, changeable, dangerously unstable.

"Oh, I don't believe so, Basil," she said. "I marry you pretty often, but tonight I don't seem to have any plans at all. You may make me a gift on your first or second, however. I always like that."

But when they had parted she asked herself: "But whom will I marry tonight?"

The panhandler was Basil Bagelbaker, who would be the richest man in the world within an hour and a half.

(Lafferty always writes in this campy style. He's truly weird.) What's especially important about the world of "Slow Tuesday Night" is that its wild acceleration of experiences that for us unfold with tortoiselike slowness—marriages, divorces, the amassing and losing of fortunes—results in a strangely *static* world. Lafferty depicts just another Tuesday night, slower than some, maybe, but not essentially different from any other evening. Thus another exchange, at the story's end, between the two characters we met at the outset:

A sleepy panhandler met Ildefonsa Impala on the way. "Preserve us this morning, Ildy," he said, "and will you marry me the coming night?"

"Likely I will, Basil," she told him. "Did you marry Judy during the night past?"

"I'm not sure."

All this was imagined decades before the internet caused us to live something resembling it. And if the claim that Lafferty's world prefigures ours strikes you as an exaggeration, I would ask you, dear reader, to remember the *next-to-last* thing that social media taught you to be outraged about. I bet you can remember only the last one. Every night on the internet is "Slow Tuesday Night."

Hartmut Rosa points out—in rather less eccentric language than Lafferty's—that our everyday experience of this acceleration has a weirdly contradictory character. On the one hand, we feel that "everything is moving so fast"— as one philosopher puts it, "Speed is the god of our era"— but often we also *simultaneously* feel trapped in our social structure and life pattern, imprisoned, deprived of meaningful choice. Think of the college student who takes classes to prepare her for a job that might not exist in a decade— but who feels that she has to take *some* classes that will look good to prospective employers. To her, there doesn't seem any escape from the need for professional self-presentation; but there also don't seem to be any reliable means to know what form that self-presentation should take. You can't stop playing the game, but its rules keep changing without warning.

It's worth noting that Francis Fukuyama wrote his notorious book about "the end of history"—arguing that we had reached "the end point of mankind's ideological evolution and the universalization of Western liberal democracy as the final form of human government"—in 1992, just as the internet age was kicking into high gear: everything is moving *so fast* . . . but history has ended. In this way, Rosa contends, we find ourselves in a state of "frenetic standstill," constantly in motion but going nowhere. Much like Ildefonsa Impala and Basil Bagelbaker.

You can readily see, I suspect, how information overload

and social acceleration work together to create a paralyzing feedback loop, pressing us to practice continually the triage I spoke of earlier, forcing our judgments about what to pay attention to, what to think about, to become ever more peremptory and irreversible. (That's one of the reasons why social media's attitude toward sinners—the unclean, the defiling—is simply to expel them from the community, so they don't need to be thought about any further.) And all this has the further effect of locking us into the present moment. There's no time to think about anything else than the *Now*, and the *not-Now* increasingly takes on the character of an unwelcome and, in its otherness, even befouling imposition.

And even if you're not inclined to feel defiled by the past, you're probably unlikely to have it presented to you— you'll have to seek it out. In a recent interview, the screenwriter and showrunner Tony Tost offered the theory that "the reason so many younger Americans have apparently no awareness of singers/movies/TV shows/writers from before their teenage years is because their parents (my generation) have been overindulgent in letting them only access culture that's directly marketed to their age group." The nearly universal availability of streaming video makes this decision, or non-decision, easier to make. "For a lot of families there's no reason to trot out the old cultural chestnuts because the newest freshest thing is right at their fingertips." Tost continues,

> So it's no wonder younger folks don't have any cultural memory or taste for aesthetic adventure. In pre-school

their parents played the most recent kids' music in the car for them instead of the older music the parents actually wanted to listen to. And at home the kids only watched kid-centric YouTube channels or superhero or Pixar movies instead of suffering through dad's weird favorite old movies. So when the kids hit elementary school, they only have ears and eyes for whatever was being marketed to their age group that year. The same thing carried forth to junior high, high school, and beyond. So at what point would they have discovered who Akira Kurosawa or Billie Holiday or even Robert Redford might be? Every step of their development they've been trapped in the pre-packaged bubble of the new.

"The pre-packaged bubble of the new" is a potent phrase. William James famously commented that "the baby, assailed by eyes, ears, nose, skin, and entrails at once, feels it all as one great blooming, buzzing confusion," but this is the character of experience for everyone whose temporal bandwidth is narrowed to *this instant*. How can we escape, or even meaningfully reckon with, the blooming, the buzzing, the confusion?

But what do I mean by "temporal bandwidth"?

If you were inclined to write a defense of studying the past, there are any number of ways you might go about it. Indeed, just as you can easily find online countless persons denouncing "all history hitherto," you can also find online countless persons denouncing this present age as woefully, shamefully ignorant of the past. Often you can identify these persons by their deployment of a famous zinger that no one is sure who coined: "Those who do not learn from the past are condemned to repeat it."

In a well-known passage from Milan Kundera's 1979 novel *The Book of Laughter and Forgetting*, one character says that "the first step in liquidating a people . . . is to erase its memory. Destroy its books, its culture, its history. Then have somebody write new books, manufacture a new culture, invent a new history. Before long the nation will begin to forget what it is and what it was." This is true, powerfully true, vitally true. I could write a book about it and feel that I had done something of value. There's also this, from the preface that the seventeenth-century philosopher Thomas Hobbes wrote to his translation of the ancient Greek historian Thucydides: "For the principle and proper work of history [is] to instruct and enable men, by the knowledge of actions past, to bear themselves prudently in the present and providentially towards the future." I cannot express too strongly how passionately I agree with this commendation of attending to the past.

However, these insights, though powerful, are not what this book is about. I will not try to convince you that a knowledge of history will protect you from the propaganda of tyrants, or sharpen your political judgment, or even help you to identify fake quotes online—though I believe that a knowledge of history will indeed produce all those good things. I am going to try to convince you that the deeper your understanding of the past, the greater *personal density* you will accumulate.

I take that phrase from one of the most infuriatingly complex and inaccessible of twentieth-century novels, Thomas Pynchon's *Gravity's Rainbow*. Fortunately, you don't have to read the novel to grasp the essential point that one of its characters makes. That character is a German engineer named Kurt Mondaugen, and his profession perhaps explains the curiously technical language he uses to express his core insight. Here is the passage in which we learn about "Mondaugen's Law":

> "Personal density," Kurt Mondaugen in his Peenemünde office not too many steps away from here, enunciating the Law which will one day bear his name, "is directly proportional to temporal bandwidth."
>
> "Temporal bandwidth" is the width of your present, your *now*. . . . The more you dwell in the past and in the future, the thicker your bandwidth, the more solid your persona. But the narrower your sense of Now, the more tenuous you are. It may get to where you're having trouble remembering what you were doing five minutes ago. . . .

We might add, in light of our earlier discussion of social acceleration, that insofar as that acceleration traps us in the moment, the more weightless we become. We lack the density to stay put even in the mildest breeze from our news feeds. Temporal bandwidth helps give us the requisite density: it addresses our condition of "frenetic standstill" by simultaneously slowing us down and giving us more freedom of movement. It is a balm for agitated souls.*

In other words, this is a self-help book.

I don't mean that as a joke. The whole idea of self-help has a bad name among intelligent people, for two major reasons. First, what we call "self-help" is often a kind of self-*soothing*, a collection of banal reassurances that you might need to adjust a few things but you don't really have to make major changes. That "Archaic Torso of Apollo" was surely exaggerating, then, when it told the poet Rilke "You must change your life." Second, much self-help operates according to a listicle model of help: These Ten Tricks Will Change Your Life! Which might work if you didn't have enormously powerful social and technological forces pushing you in directions you don't get to choose. And if you weren't so light, so lacking in density, that you can't retain your place when the winds start blowing, even if you want to.

The German sociologist Gerd-Günter Voss has outlined the development, over many centuries, of three forms of the "conduct of life." The first is the *traditional*: in this model your life takes the form that the lives of people in your culture and class have always taken, at least for as long as anyone remembers. The key values in the traditional

---

*John Dewey articulated a very similar thought more than a century ago: "A society which is mobile, which is full of channels for the distribution of a change occurring anywhere, must see to it that its members are educated to personal initiative and adaptability. Otherwise, they will be overwhelmed by the changes in which they are caught and whose significance or connections they do not perceive. The result will be a confusion in which a few will appropriate to themselves the results of the blind and externally directed activities of others." *Democracy and Education: An Introduction to the Philosophy of Education* (New York: Macmillan, 1916).

conduct of life are "security and regularity." The second model is the *strategic*: people who follow this model have clear goals in mind (first, to get into an elite university; later, to become a radiologist or own their own company or retire at fifty) and form a detailed strategic plan to achieve those goals. But, Voss suggests, those two, while still present in various parts of the world, are increasingly being displaced by a third model for the conduct of life: the *situational*.

The situational model has arisen in recent social orders that are unprecedentedly dynamic and fluid. People are less likely to plan to be radiologists when they hear that radiologists may be replaced by computers. They are less likely to plan to own a company when whatever business they're inclined toward may not exist in a decade, or may undergo some kind of transformation we can't currently anticipate. They are less likely to plan to have children when they don't know what kind of world (in terms of climate as well as society and technology) they will be raising those children in. They might not even want to plan to have dinner with a friend a week from Friday, because who knows what better options might turn up between now and then?

Though the situational conduct of life is clearly distinct from the strategic model, it's a kind of strategy all the same: a way of coping with social acceleration. But it's also, or threatens to be, a kind of abandonment of serious reflection on what makes life good. It's a principled refusal to ask, with Horace, "Where is it virtue comes from, is it from books?" or "What is the way to become a friend to yourself?" You end up just managing the moment. Therefore you certainly won't ask whether your life will be driven by "hope and fear about trivial things, / In anxious alternation in your mind"—because what else could possibly drive it?

Hartmut Rosa points out that there is a close relationship between these common current experiences—of "social acceleration," of time being somehow out of joint, of having access only to a "situational" conduct of life—and anxiety and depression. The feeling of being at a "frenetic standstill" is highly characteristic of the depressed person. I do not wish to suggest that reading old books is a cure for depression; but the development of personal density, to which reading old books can be a vital contribution, just might be a hedge against depressive inclinations, might provide—we will see this more than once in the pages that follow—a port, for however brief a time, in the storm.

Because when the storm—the storm that carries what Rudyard Kipling called the "wind-borne Gods of the Market Place," the gods who push us about but are themselves pushed by still greater forces that they don't control—blows the fragile dinghy of your self across the great sea, one day you'll wake up and wonder how you ended up where you are, where you never wanted to be, where you'd rather not be. No, you'll then think, the purely situational is no way to live. You can't make a virtue out of *that* necessity, no matter how quickly things change, because those currents will always be more agile than you are, and more purposeful too. (There are many, many people paid very well indeed to write the code that determines what your situations are and how you will respond to them. They are highly placed among the Gods of the Market Place.) You *need* the personal density that will hold you firmly until, in *your* considered and settled judgment, it is time to move. And to acquire the requisite density you have to get out of your transitory moment and into bigger time. Personal density is proportionate to temporal bandwidth.

I am aware that I have taken on a difficult task here: attention to the past is a hard sell. I want to argue that you can't understand the place and time you're in by immersion; the opposite's true. You have to step out and away and back and forward, and you have to do it regularly. Then you come back to the here and now, and say: Ah. That's how it is. But maybe 2 percent of the people I encounter are willing even to think about this possibility. The other 98 percent are wholly creatures of this particular intersection in space-time, and can't be made to care about anything else. I'm writing for the 2 percent. But even for *them* this is a hard sell. It is a profound struggle to overcome the gravitational pull of the moment, to achieve escape velocity from presentism.

Many factors make that gravitational pull so strong, and we've already seen a few. Tony Tost, in the interview I quoted earlier, is especially concerned with the effects of presentism on children, and thinks that we ought to make them watch stuff not made for them, not marketed to them, not fired like an arrow at their amygdalae: "Older and adult art forces them to get out of their comfort zone and deal with a little ambiguity and thematic density and encounter shit that wasn't manufactured for their immediate effortless consumption." Tost comes pretty close to making the very argument I am making here: Exposing kids to "older and adult art" teaches them "to find value and pleasure in something that wasn't necessarily made for them. I think that's healthy as hell." And insofar as we fail to give children this challenge, this opportunity, Tost continues, "I'm afraid we're producing emptier, more fragile, less intellectually and aesthetically adventurous adults." Lacking in *personal density*, one might say—and for that very reason vulnerable. Nassim Nicholas Taleb describes the strange natural phenomenon of *antifragility*—"Some things benefit from shocks; they thrive and grow when exposed to volatility, randomness, disorder, and stressors and love adventure, risk, and uncertainty"—and surely we'd all love to help children become antifragile in this way. A powerful instrument in generating that antifragility is a serious encounter with the past—but that's what YouTube recommendations and an online world of "You May Also Like" make very difficult to see. So, in listing the impediments to achieving such density, we can add to the forces I have described algorithmically targeted marketing.

It's a forbidding package. And there's one more key element to this package I want to identify: the peculiar way in which our present-mindedness is determined by our historical consciousness, our awareness that eras of history *differ* from one another in ways that can't be altered. As the philosopher Charles Taylor has suggested, one of the oddest elements of our presentism is that it is based on a historical thesis: "it is a crucial fact of our present spiritual predicament that it is historical; that is, our understanding of ourselves and where we stand is partly defined by our sense of having come to where we are, of having overcome a previous condition."

Taylor writes this in the context of talking about what it's like to live in a "disenchanted world," a world governed not by spirits and demons but by the immutable laws of nature. On some level we know "that it was a struggle and an achievement to get to where we are; and that in some respects this achievement is fragile." Moreover,

> We know this because each one of us as we grew up has had to take on the disciplines of disenchantment, and we regularly reproach each other for our failings in this regard, and accuse each other of "magical" thinking, of indulging in "myth," of giving way to "fantasy"; we say that X isn't living in our century, that Y has a "mediae-val" mind, while Z, whom we admire, is way ahead of her time.

If Taylor is right, then we have an incentive to avoid looking at the past, or to look at it only with condescension. We believe in progress, we believe that history really does have an arc and that it bends toward justice. It's a very comfort-ing thing to believe, and we don't want to look into the past only to discover that we have lost sight of vital truths and wise practices. Christopher Hitchens, in describing what he believes to be the baleful history of what he calls "religion," celebrates the power to "escape the gnarled hands which reach out to drag us back to the catacombs and the reeking altars and the guilty pleasures of subjection and abjection." This is not far from how many people feel about the *whole* of the past: that if we're not careful we could be dragged back toward it. (That fear is the source of the power of stories like *The Handmaid's Tale*, in its novelistic but especially in its filmed form. The past as undead, as revenant.)

So when you sum together these presentist forces— information overload, social acceleration, pervasive algorithmic marketing, a historical awareness that celebrates progress and escape—it is difficult to push back against them. Much of this book does indeed push back, and argues for an account of the past that emphasizes its treasures more than its threats; but that positive work can't really begin until we get a better understanding of our resistance to the voices of those who came before us.

2.

TABLE FELLOWSHIP

The project of increasing temporal bandwidth that I recommend here requires the opening of our minds and hearts to people from the past so that they stand before us three-dimensionally, in all the ways they resemble us and all the ways they do not. Thus I invoke in this book's title a line often uttered by the poet W. H. Auden: "Art is our chief means of breaking bread with the dead." *Breaking bread* is at the heart of this project: sitting at table with our ancestors and learning to know them in their difference from, as well as their likeness to, us.

"Table fellowship" was a vexed issue in the ancient world, nowhere more so than among Jews, who had, and of course often still have, elaborate laws regarding food and drink. One of the many points that made Jesus of Nazareth controversial among his fellow Jews was his declaration that all foods are clean. In the book of Acts we are told that the apostle Peter had a kind of vision in which he saw animals of every kind and was told by a disembodied voice to eat them; and when Peter, as an observant Jew, demurred, the voice said to him, "What God has made clean, you must not call profane."

But old habits die hard—as does the feeling that the presence of certain other people, and their food, can make a person unclean, can *defile*. Thus Peter's reluctance to accept his vision—and thus the insistence, in the Clementine Homilies, a third-century document widely read by Christians, that that vision was wrong: "We do not . . . take our food from the same table as Gentiles, inasmuch as we cannot eat along with them, because they live impurely . . . our religion compels us to make a distinction." Who says this? According to the text, Peter—the same Peter who, in the book of Acts, came to the opposite conclusion. The Clementine Homilies are a pious fiction, but they tell us something about the felt need to separate from those who "live impurely"—"for our religion compels us to make a distinction."

Fortunately, we live in an enlightened society that has transcended such irrational narrowness and exclusivity. Right?

Perhaps not so much. We are certainly still concerned with the clean and the unclean. Consider this recent phenomenon: restaurant diners discovering that a politician or media personality from the Other Side is eating at a nearby table, and agitating to have the offender cast out. We might also think of people who won't sit at Thanksgiving or Christmas or Passover dinner with those whose politics are simply too alien, too repulsive: and note that it's not being in the same *room* that defiles so much as sharing a *meal*. As the Clementine Homilies say, "when we have persuaded them to have true thoughts, and to follow a right course of action, . . . then we dwell with them."

If we cannot break bread with our contemporaries who violate our political commitments—whose views seem so alien and wrong that to share a meal with them feels like a kind of defilement—then it would seem that asking us to break bread with the dead is a futile act indeed. But perhaps not.

The dead, being dead, speak only at our invitation: they will not come uninvited to our table. They are at our mercy, like that flock of shades who gather around Odysseus when he comes as a living man to the land of Hades: they remain silent until their tongues are touched with the blood of the living. What the dead we encounter in books demand is only the blood of our attention, which we are free to withhold.

My plea is that we do *not* withhold it, that we use our power to give them utterance. We can always, if they shock or offend us too greatly, turn aside and render them silent again. And there is a good chance that they *will* shock us. I want to stress here, and will stress again as we move on, the vital necessity of *difference*. There is a kind of book about the past that proclaims the value of studying our ancestors, but does so by insisting that the really useful and interesting ones are remarkably like us. So in *The Swerve*, Stephen Greenblatt's book about the recovery by Poggio Bracciolini, in the early modern period, of the writings of the ancient philosopher-poet Lucretius, we get heroes who are scarcely distinguishable from Stephen Greenblatt and who, conveniently, have all the same enemies.* The Jesus of Laurie Beth Jones's *Jesus, CEO* will give bosses plenty of advice for how to manage disgruntled underlings but, you may be sure, will never say, "Sell all you have and give it to the poor." The popularity in recent years of ancient Stoicism is possible in part because the Stoicism so retrieved doesn't ask us to change any of our current beliefs, only a few of our practices. (We'll hear more about this later.)

The British historian David Cannadine has written a book called *The Undivided Past: Humanity Beyond Our Differences* that, quite commendably, seeks to push back against the many different forms of identity politics, from the right and the left alike, that overemphasize whatever divides us from one another in order to gain some political or social leverage. Cannadine argues that "there is a case for taking a broader, more ecumenical, and even more optimistic view of human identities and relations." This view "accepts difference and conflict based on clashing sectional identities," but wants to push beyond that to see "affinities" and to promote "conversations across these allegedly impermeable boundaries of identity, which embody and express a broader sense of humanity that goes beyond our dissimilarities." Cannadine approvingly quotes Maya Angelou:

---

*As the medievalist Laura Saetveit Miles noted, Greenblatt's book "relies on a narrative of good guys (Poggio, as well as Lucretius) defeating bad guys and thus bringing forth a glorious transformation. This is dangerous not only because it is inaccurate but, more importantly, because it subscribes to a progressivist model of history that insists on the onward march of society, a model that all too easily excuses the crimes and injustices of modernity." https://www.vox.com/2016/7/20/12216712/harvard-professor-the-swerve-greenblatt-middle-ages-false.

I note the obvious differences
Between each sort and type,
But we are more alike, my friends,
Than we are unalike.

I devoutly hope that this is true, and that it is true of those with whom we connect across time as well as across space and social class and race and sex. But I believe that any significant increase in personal density is largely achieved through encounters with un-likeness.

The real challenge, but also the real opportunity, of breaking bread with the dead comes when the dead say something that freaks us out—freaks us out to the point that we are strongly tempted to turn away in disgust and horror. But those may be just the moments when we need to steel ourselves to keep giving the blood of our attention.

In some contexts we understand this: think of the (now quite long) history of arguments to recognize "the other," to seek out and respect otherness, to hear unheard and un-noticed voices from marginalized communities or groups. People in my line of work have been beating this drum for a long time. To take one vivid example, consider the cultural theorist Donna Haraway's recent book *Staying with the Trouble: Making Kin in the Chthulucene*, an argument for, in politically vexed times, "staying with the trouble and for making generative oddkin." (I know that there's some fancy academic language here but please bear with me—please stay with the trouble.)

"Making generative oddkin"? By that, Haraway means

seeking to forge kinship bonds with all sorts of creatures and things—pigeons, for instance. There's a fascinating early chapter in her book on human interaction with pigeons. Of course, that interaction has been conducted largely on human terms, and Haraway wants to create two-way streets where in the past these paths ran only from humans to everything else. How to get the pigeons to participate willingly in such a project is a question without an obvious answer, but it's a question that Haraway feels we must ask, because "staying with the trouble requires making oddkin; that is, we require each other in unexpected collaborations and combinations, in hot compost piles. We become-with each other or not at all."*

But here's the complication: Who gets included in "each other"? Besides pigeons, I mean. Haraway says explicitly that her *human* kin are "antiracist, anticolonial, anticapitalist, proqueer feminists of every color and from every people," and people who share her commitment to "Make Kin Not Babies": "Pronatalism in all its powerful guises ought to be in question almost everywhere."

I suspect that—to borrow a tripartite distinction from the psychiatrist and blogger Scott Alexander—most people who use that kind of language are fine with their *in-group* ("antiracist, anticolonial, anticapitalist, proqueer feminists of every color and from every people") and fine with the *fargroup* (pigeons), but the *outgroup*? The outgroup that lives in your city and votes in the same elections you do?

---

*Soon after writing this passage I came across a wonderful new book by Jon Day called *Homing: On Pigeons, Dwellings and Why We Return* (London: Hodder & Stoughton, 2019). In it he quotes Donna Haraway, which I suppose brings things full circle.

Maybe not so much. Does the project of making kin extend to that couple down the street from you who have five kids, who attend a big-box evangelical church, and who voted for the wrong person in the last presidential election? And who, moreover, are a little more likely to talk back than pigeons are? (Even assuming that they might be interested in making kin with Donna Haraway, which, let's face it, is equally unlikely. Presumably they too would be more comfortable with the pigeons.)

Here, I think, is where my project of increasing temporal bandwidth comes in: it is a way of making kin that is a little less demanding and threatening than dealing with those weirdo neighbors—at least, if we think about the project in the right way.

In 2019 the novelist and teacher Brian Morton published a fascinating essay about his encounter with a student who had tried reading Edith Wharton's 1905 novel *The House of Mirth* but after fifty pages threw it in the trash. What he believed—rightly—to be Wharton's overt anti-Semitism, exemplified in a character named Simon Rosedale, appalled him. Throughout the novel Rosedale exhibits, or is thought by the heroine, Lily Bart, to exhibit, an unsettling combination of deference and arrogance, thus this characteristic sentence: "He knew he should have to go slowly, and the instincts of his race fitted him to suffer rebuffs and put up with delays." The student was justifiably appalled by Wharton's lofty contempt for Rosedale and said, "I don't want anyone like that in my house." We might say that the student could not abide having table fellowship with a writer so overtly and unapologetically bigoted.

As Morton reflected on this encounter, later, he came to believe that—whether or not the student was right to stop reading Wharton's book—the phrase "I don't want anyone like that in my house" reflected a misconception. "It's as if we imagine an old book to be a time machine that brings the writer to *us*. We buy a book and take it home, and the writer appears before us, asking to be admitted into our company. If we find that the writer's views are ethnocentric or sexist or racist, we reject the application, and we bar his or her entry into the present." But no, thought Morton: "it isn't the writer who's the time traveler. It's the reader. When we pick up an old novel, we're not bringing the novelist into our world and deciding whether he or she is enlightened enough to belong here; we're journeying into the novelist's world and taking a look around." The author is not a guest at *our* table; we are a guest at *hers*.

It's a lovely metaphor, but (like all metaphors) limited, because if we're *literally* sitting at someone's table it can be difficult to get away without offense or embarrassment. There are many wonderful things about books, but among the most wonderful is that you can close them when you need to, when they become a little too strange, too disturbing. It's like being able to quit someone's table instantaneously but without causing trouble or offense. And the fact that you *can* escape so easily might actually be a good reason *not to*.

Let's think again about "making oddkin." We could have a very long conversation about whether it is easy, or hard, or impossible to forge genuine kinship with animals, especially nondomesticated animals. It's something people have thought about often, including some philosophers. Wittgenstein was definitively negative about the whole project: "If a lion could speak, we could not understand him." Thomas Nagel was not so sure, and wrote a later-to-be-famous essay called "What Is It Like to Be a Bat?" For a more down-to-earth exploration you might want to read Helen Macdonald's remarkable memoir *H Is for Hawk*. But whether it's possible to make such oddkin or not, we know what drives the pursuit: a profound desire to engage and reckon with otherness, without eliminating that otherness. Any discomfort we experience is very much to the point. Indeed, the *loss* of otherness may be a bad sign, as Helen Macdonald learned as, in her grief over the death of her father, she drew closer and closer to her goshawk Mabel:

> In hunting with Mabel, day after day, I had assumed—in my imagination, of course, but that was all it could ever be—her alien perspective, her inhuman understanding of the world. It brought something akin to madness, and I did not understand what I had done. When I was small I'd thought turning into a hawk would be a magical thing. What I'd read in [T. H. White's Arthurian fantasy] *The Sword in the Stone* encouraged me to think it, too, as a good and instructive thing; a lesson in life for the child who would be king. But now the lesson was killing me. It was not at all the same.

For a human to assume an "inhuman understanding of the world" is, necessarily, "something akin to madness." Mental health lies in seeking difference but always knowing it *as* difference—not collapsing my identity into that of some-one, or something, else.

And this is also true of any legitimate interest in the past. Reading old books is an education in reckoning with otherness; its hope is to make the other not identical with me but rather, in a sense, my *neighbor*. I happen to think that this kind of training is useful in helping me learn to deal with my actual on-the-ground neighbors, though that claim is not central to my argument here, and in any case there's nothing inevitable about this transfer: I know peo-ple who are exquisitely sensitive readers of texts who are also habitually rude to the people who serve them at res-taurants. But surely to encounter texts from the past is a relatively nonthreatening, and yet potentially enormously re-warding, way to practice encountering difference.

The French thinker Simone Weil believed this strongly. Weil—who was a very strange kind of religious mystic—believed that in all of our human encounters we should be seeking to discern what is eternally true. She also believed that that is hard to do when we're dealing with our actual neighbor, because our emotions tend to be so near the sur-face. (This is why it's easier for Donna Haraway and the pronatalists down her street to encounter pigeons than one another.) Weil says that "the past offers us a partially com-pleted discrimination"—an odd phrase, but a vital one. She means that the events and the persons of the past are *relatively* fully shaped—not totally complete, because the consequences of the past live on in the present, but *par-tially* so, complete enough that we can step back and take an appraising look, rather as a painter does when she's almost finished with her canvas. We do not have the same intensity of involvement in the past that we do in the present, and it's precisely that which makes the past useful to us: "Our attachments and our passions do not so thickly obscure our discrimination of the eternal in the past."

Let me try to illustrate what I think Weil means. One of the most beautiful novels I know is *Clear Light of Day* (1980), by the Indian writer Anita Desai. The story concerns the four siblings of the Das family, who live in Old Delhi, and how their lives change from the 1940s to the 1970s. Certain complex familial dynamics tend to pull them apart, to set them at odds with one another, but all of their tensions are dramatically exacerbated by the independence and subsequent partition of India in 1947. In addition to the tensions felt by all in that time and place, the Dases must deal with the uncomfortable fact that the man from whom they rent their house, Hyder Ali, is Muslim—and the family's older brother, Raja, is drawn more and more deeply into Muslim culture and the Urdu language (which he considers aesthetically superior to his family's native Hindi). When, during partition, Muslims are leaving India and Hindus are leaving the newly created state of Pakistan, and new outbreaks of violence between the groups occur every day, Raja's inclinations are fraught with strain and stress for himself and his family.

Raja eventually escapes Old Delhi, as does his sister Tara, who marries a diplomat and so lives largely overseas. The other sister, Bimla, is therefore left at home to care for her autistic brother, Baba, and watch over the gradual deterioration of their house, their neighborhood, their city—and the family that the Dases once were. As the novel progresses her bitterness grows and grows, until it generates a crisis that I will not describe here, because I very much want you to read the novel.

But here comes a spoiler I cannot avoid. At one point in the story Bim finds that she cannot sleep, and takes a book, at random, from her bookcase. It is the *Life of Aurangzeb*— the last great Mughal (and therefore Muslim) emperor of India. When the emperor knew he was dying, he dictated a letter to a close friend in which he wrote, "Now I am going alone. I grieve for your helplessness, but what is the use? Every torment I have inflicted, every sin I have committed, every wrong I have done, I carry the consequences with me. Strange that I came with nothing into the world, and now go away with this stupendous caravan of sin!"

Aurangzeb was not an indulgent or permissive monarch. His persecution of not just non-Muslims but also Muslims who understood their faith differently than he did created much anger against him, and he spent too many years of his long rule putting down rebellions for which his own intolerance was largely responsible. Given how much of her own life has been shaped, and not for good, by conflicts with Muslims, Bim might not be thought the ideal reader of his story. And yet, once she has read the words I just quoted, Desai tells us this: "Bim's mind seemed stilled at last." In absolute calm Bim realizes that she too carries a stupendous caravan of sin, one that she greatly desires to empty, as best she can.

It is the hand of time, I think, that smooths over the differences, that allows Bim to set aside all that might separate her from this Mughal emperor. She probably could have drawn no nourishment from the letters of her landlord Hyder Ali, even if they had been equally eloquent. But the buffer of the centuries enables her to see Aurangzeb as, simply, an old man who looked back over a long life with no satisfaction and much shame; and therefore to see him as someone worthy of her sympathy—someone in whose very shoes she could imagine herself. And this imaginative participation across the gap of years, of religion, of sex, settles her restless mind because it enables her to see her own situation with a clarity that's all the more powerful because it was unlooked-for.

Later on, when Bim meets with her sister Tara, she makes an apology that Tara brushes away—"it was all so long ago." To which Bim replies that, even so, "it's never over. Nothing's *over*, ever." And this is both a blessing and a curse. The past that ties us to people in ways that hurt us also ties us to people in ways that make healing possible. Sometimes we wish that the past *could* be over; sometimes we are grateful that it is not. It stands in the middle, "partially completed" but not *over*, poised between radical otherness and utter likeness. And that is why, as Weil says, "Our attachments and our passions do not so thickly obscure our discrimination of the eternal in the past." We can see what really matters—"the eternal," what *always* matters— because of that middle distance.

When we look to the past, Weil believes, what we are

always looking for is whatever "is better than we are." Some of us tend to look toward the future for what is better, but Weil thinks that "what is better than we are cannot be found in the future." The reason is simply that the future does not exist. "The future is empty and is filled by our imagination. Our imagination can only picture a perfection on our own scale. It is just as imperfect as we are; it does not surpass us by a single hair's breadth." This brings to mind the old line about the great limitation of travel: Wherever you go, there you are. The future cannot teach us because *we* are the ones who must imagine it.

I n 1996 a group of people including the musician Brian Eno, the computer scientist Danny Hillis, and the visionary Stewart Brand started the Long Now Foundation for the purpose of encouraging people to look toward the distant future. Says the foundation's website: "The Long Now Foundation hopes to provide a counterpoint to today's accelerating culture and help make long-term thinking more common. We hope to foster responsibility in the framework of the next 10,000 years." As Eno has written, "If we want to contribute to some sort of tenable future, we have to reach a frame of mind where it comes to seem unacceptable—gauche, uncivilised—to act in disregard of our descendants." Amen to that, and amen again. But if Weil is right, our ability to think toward the future is limited by our deficient imaginations, and therefore we need the witness of the *past*. Temporal bandwidth needs to be extended in both directions. Better to look five thousand years forward *and* five thousand years backward rather than strain to see only the future, which, being nonexistent, cannot *resist* us. The past, by contrast, tells of what we need to know but would never think to look for.

Weil believes that for those who wish to encounter the eternal, to find something better than ourselves, writings from the past are useful because "the mere passing of time effects a certain separation between what is eternal and what is not"; which is her reason for saying, as earlier noted, Our attachments and our passions do not so thickly obscure our discrimination of the eternal in the past as in the present." And, she adds, especially useful to us is "the past which is temporally so dead that it offers no food for our passions."

This is why Bim could draw nourishment from the dying words of Aurangzeb, and why, I believe, at the outbreak of the Second World War, Weil wrote an essay about the *Iliad*—one of the most famous, and indeed one of the most powerful, things ever written about Homer's great poem.

Weil reads the *Iliad* as someone who is preoccupied, indeed obsessed, by what she calls "force": "that x that turns anybody who is subjected to it into a thing." She is watching force sweep across Europe, driving people—including Weil's parents, who escaped Paris, and then France itself, ending up spending the war in New York—out of their homes, and turning millions of them into the final "thing": a corpse. It is this horrible transformation of living persons into things that "the *Iliad* never tires of showing us."

For those dreamers who considered that force, thanks to progress, would soon be a thing of the past, the *Iliad* could appear as an historical document; for others, whose powers of recognition are more acute and who perceive force, today as yesterday, at the very center of human history, the *Iliad* is the purest and the loveliest of mirrors.

But why look so far into the past for this revelatory mirror? The First World War had destroyed many of the young men of Europe just twenty years earlier, and had produced a great outpouring of fiction and poetry and memoir. Why not read *those* books?

Indeed, many of those books are worth reading; some of them are masterpieces. But, in a strange sense, their very ability to engage the emotions of readers in 1940 limits their revelatory power. Many readers of Weil's time remembered the Great War (as they called it); their fathers or brothers or lovers or sons fought in it, and often enough died. Stories about that war could show to the readers of 1940 some of the peculiar horrors of their century; but what they could not show, not in the way that the *Iliad* does, is the cold, terrible fact that force lies, "today as yesterday, at the very center of human history." When Andromache pleads with Hector not to return to the fighting, when Achilles weeps and rages over the death of his beloved friend Patroclus, when old King Priam goes to his knees to beg his son's killer for his son's body, a powerful electrical current leaps across the millennia, from that distant pole to our immediate one. Such a strange world, such an alien world; yet its occupants, too, know the implacable rule of force. Something terrible links, without erasing the differences between, the heights of ancient Troy and the cold beaches of Normandy. That linkage illuminates, reveals, the strange continuities of history, but only by keeping otherness before us as well. *That* is what makes the *Iliad* "the loveliest of mirrors."

3

The Sins of the Past

—=····⟨⟨·⟩⟩···=—

B ut is reading the *Iliad* worth it? In order to get this wisdom of the past that Simone Weil thinks so highly of, are we supposed to ignore——or worse, *accept*——a world in which masculine hyperaggression is celebrated and women are treated merely as "prizes"? Doesn't the whole story kick off because Agamemnon takes away Achilles's prize and Achilles pouts about it? Are we simply to set aside our modern beliefs that women are human beings?

In a word: no. In more words:

Many times over the years I have read, or heard, people encouraging readers of old books to set aside their modern assumptions in order to enter into the world of the old text. I think this is bad advice. Does anyone really think that women reading Shakespeare's *The Taming of the Shrew* should "set aside" their belief that women are not here to be "tamed" by masterful men? Should we ask them to consider whether Petruchio's point of view might not be right after all? No: but what we need to do is keep *all* our values in play, not just *some* of them.

Let me return here to Brian Morton's essay about his student's horror at the anti-Semitism of Edith Wharton, and his recommendation that we think of ourselves as travelers into the past, chrono-anthropologists studying strange cultures. He thinks that with that scholarly distance we might be able to see not just Wharton's anti-Semitism but also "the riches she had to offer——her aphoristic wit; her astonishingly well-wrought sentences; her subtle sense of how moral strength and weakness coexist in each of us; her criticisms of the cruelties of her historical moment, which are not unlike the cruelties of ours." And we might even be able to "see that although Wharton held many views that were reactionary even then, . . . she was ahead of her time in other ways, particularly in her awareness of how women of her era were suffocated by the social roles imposed on them."

We will, of course, sometimes ask ourselves how a person could be so incisively critical of some injustices while being so utterly blind to others——but then, don't we also think that about people we meet today? Isn't this strange mixture of vices and virtues, foolishness and wisdom, blindness and insight, simply the human condition? (And, if we're going to be honest about it, *my* condition, and yours?)

One of the pleasant side effects of our current presentism, and its disdain for our ancestors, is that it has called forth responses like that of Morton's. It has caused people who love (at least some of) the works of the past to acknowledge the current call to name injustice for what it is while denying that that calls for old books to be thrown in the trash, or simply ignored. Another intelligent response comes from the English philosopher Julian Baggini, who recently wrote:

> Admiring the great thinkers of the past has become morally hazardous. Praise Immanuel Kant, and you might be reminded that he believed that "Humanity is at its greatest perfection in the race of the whites," and "the yellow Indians do have a meagre talent." Laud Aristotle, and you'll have to explain how a genuine sage could have thought that "the male is by nature superior and the female inferior, the male ruler and the female subject." Write a eulogy to David Hume, as I recently did here, and you will be attacked for singing the praises of someone who wrote in 1753–54: "I am apt to suspect the Negroes, and in general all other species of men . . . to be naturally inferior to the whites."

Looking at those appalling quotations, which appear at the very outset of Baggini's essay, I cannot but admire him for so firmly grasping the nettle. He is not hiding from us, or even minimizing, the vices of the people he wants to defend.

Baggini's chief argument is that none of these figures had the good fortune to be confronted with eloquent proponents of opposing views. They did not have the benefit that we have of being able to read Mary Wollstonecraft and Virginia Woolf and Frederick Douglass and Martin Luther King Jr. "Becoming aware that even the likes of Kant and Hume were products of their times is a humbling reminder that the greatest minds can still be blind to mistakes and evils, if they are widespread enough." And a reminder also of how extraordinary were the gifts and the courage of those who, like Wollstonecraft and Douglass and so many others, managed to cut their way through thickets of convention that so reliably trap ordinary folks—and sometimes even great geniuses.

We can understand how those thickets of convention grow so large and strong by reflecting on our earlier discussion of informational triage. Nobody thinks about everything; nobody *can* think about everything; our cognitive limitations are such that there will always be a great many topics that we will take no real thought over, but will simply believe what the people around us, for the most part, believe. These views can scarcely be dignified by the term "belief": they're more like the intellectual equivalent of ambient noise, always there in the background but never noticed, never brought to consciousness for reflection.

Here's an example: there will be a time, I am certain, when our descendants will be positively aghast that we ever ate animals. How could we *possibly* have been so thoughtlessly cruel? What could we say for ourselves, should someone from the future travel back in time and shake an admonitory finger at us? If she came to our moment, the vegetarians and vegans among us would crow in triumph as the rest of us muttered excuses. And what we'd probably say was that we never really thought it through, that we were raised eating meat, it was what we had always done, the restaurants were full of meat dishes, trying to go vegetarian seemed sort of daunting, we always had other things to think about that took higher priority—that last point above all. And we would say those things to the visitor of the future because those are the things we have been saying to ourselves for a very long time.

But imagine that visitor from the future going back to, say, London in the year 1500, a place and time in which vegetarianism had scarcely been heard of and veganism altogether unknown. (In south India the story is rather different.) Would those people even be able to make sense of the visitor's admonition? Certain cultural circumstances have to be in place for us even to entertain alternatives to our standard practices. Thus this recent thought from the philosopher Thomas Nagel in *The New York Review of Books*:

> Whether we should kill animals for food is one of the deepest disagreements of our time; but we should not be surprised if the issue is rendered moot within the next few decades, when cultured meat (also called clean meat, synthetic meat, or in vitro meat) becomes less expensive to produce than meat from slaughtered animals, and equally palatable. When that happens, I suspect that our present practices, being no longer gastronomically necessary, will suddenly become morally unimaginable.

That is, certain moral judgments will be easily reached when technology *makes* them easily reachable. Being a vegan is a great deal more challenging when the only vegetables you have are the ones that can be grown within fifteen miles of your cottage. When technology doesn't promote certain admirable choices, we struggle. We practice triage. We put some decisions at the top of our list and others much further down. As John Dewey wrote a century ago, "It seems almost incredible to us, for example, that things which we know very well, could have escaped recognition in past ages. We incline to account for it by attributing congenital stupidity to our forerunners and by assuming superior native intelligence on our own part. But the explanation is that their modes of life did not call for attention to such facts, but held their minds riveted to other things."

Nevertheless: we all need better strategies for making decisions, because the *defaults* we have inherited have costs that we are rarely aware of—and one of the purposes of this book is to increase our awareness of those costs. Just as our word-processing program gives us a default font that we might not have the energy to change, and a digital thermostat offers preset temperatures that we might not be sure how to change, our social media feeds assume that we will be interested in . . . what everyone else is interested in, which will surely be something that happened today. We may not know that we *can* change the default settings of the media machine; we may know but lack the time and energy to do so. And so those settings continue to *reinforce* the presentism that they're claiming merely to *reflect*. By reading and considering the past, we cut through the thick, strong vines that bind our attention to the things of the moment. Our attention thereby becomes more free.

Several years ago, the blogger and technologist Alyssa Vance made an extremely useful distinction: between positive and negative selection. Vance points out that when you're in the selection business—for example, trying to pick players for a sports team—you can focus on what your candidates are *able* to do, which is positive selection, or what they're *unable* to do, which is negative selection. Positive selection is about encouraging the good, negative selection about eliminating the bad. Vance thinks that academic life, to take one social institution among many, is built around negative selection. What's at stake might be admission to an undergraduate institution, or admission to a graduate program, or a postdoctoral fellowship, or a faculty position, or tenure, or a promotion, but in each case the logic is generally the same: find the shortcomings of candidates, any old shortcomings, so you can send them to the reject pile. Vance doesn't say this, but I believe that in any situation that requires a lot of informational triage—which is to say, any situation that occurs in conditions of information overload and social acceleration—we default to negative selection. It makes our lives as selectors *so* much easier.

Scott Alexander has shrewdly applied Vance's distinction to how we think about figures from the past and has pointed out how costly it is: If we follow the practice of negative selection we'll dismiss Isaac Newton because he had weird and wrong ideas about secret messages in the Bible. Similarly, we'll dismiss Edith Wharton because of her anti-Semitism, David Hume because of his racism, and Aristotle because of his sexism. The pool of candidates for our attention will get smaller and smaller—which is, after all, what negative selection is meant to do—but there's a point at which a hyperdeveloped feature can become a bug. That pool of candidates is getting smaller, but perhaps *too* small; and certainly the writers or books in that pool are getting narrower and narrower in the scope of their minds.

Eventually we get a nicely manageable collection of ideas, all of which are more or less the same.

Again: we *should* judge characters from the past in precisely the same way we judge characters of our own time, according to whether we think their behavior is good or bad, virtuous or vicious. (The viewer who calls Petruchio's treatment of Kate abusive is *not wrong*. The reader who says that Hume was straightforwardly racist is *not wrong*.) My problem with the disregard of the past that we typically manifest today is that we are highly selective in what elements of a historical person's character we are willing to take seriously. We tend to consider only those elements that reflect the dominant concerns of our moment, which are not the only concerns that are relevant to human judgment. In looking at figures from the past, we behave, as Vance and Alexander suggest, rather like admissions officers at elite colleges and universities: We look for ways to send them to the reject pile. And we do this for exactly the same reason that college admissions officers do. We are overwhelmed by data, we are continually at the mercy of a fire hose of information, and anything we can do to limit the amount of data that we have to deal with, we do. It's understandable, but it's unfair and unjust. As people who work with prisoners often say, no one should be defined by the worst thing that they ever did. We need to look at the whole person, and if we do our task becomes more complex, but also more rewarding.

Consider in this light the Founders of the United States. It seems to me that what we ought to say about them is that they rarely understood the full implications of their best ideas. There's no doubt that Washington and Jefferson should have realized that the practice of slavery was completely incompatible with the ideals they put forth in the Declaration of Independence and then, later, in the Constitution. But if they had not articulated those ideals so powerfully, it is likely that slavery would have been less frequently challenged, less often scorned—socially stronger. It must be remembered that the core ideas themselves—that all human beings are created equal, that social differentiation and social hierarchy are *not* written into the fabric of the universe—were scarcely taken for granted at the time that the Declaration of Independence was composed. Indeed, they were hotly contested by those who believed that royalty and aristocracy—and the legal as well as social superiority of royals and aristocrats to the lower classes—were ordained by God.

Or consider one of the most famous and lastingly influential of political pamphlets, the one whose full title is *Areopagitica; A Speech of Mr. John Milton for the Liberty of Unlicenc'd Printing, to the Parlament of England* (published in 1644—despite the title it wasn't a speech). There Milton makes a rigorously logical and deeply impassioned plea for the freedom to express even the most outrageous political ideas—for, the poet argued, when "books freely permitted are," this freedom conduces "both to the trial of virtue and the exercise of truth." It is surely "more wholesome, more prudent, and more Christian that many be tolerated, rather than all compelled."

Marvelous! Beautiful! Persuasive!—and then the very next sentence Milton writes is "I mean not tolerated

Popery, and open superstition, which as it extirpates all religions and civil supremacies, so itself should be extirpate...."
Ah. So no freedom of printing for Catholics. Moreover, he continues, "that also which is impious or evil absolutely either against faith or manners no law can possibly permit, that intends not to unlaw itself"—at which point we must wonder what actually *could* be published in Milton's regime of freedom.

And yet, *Areopagitica* was a rather extreme argument in its time. King Charles I had recently been driven out of London by forces loyal to Parliament, and Parliament was dominated by Milton's kind of Protestant Christians: men deeply suspicious of the Church of England's episcopal (that is, bishop-led) order, men who had lived in fear of the royal courts that suppressed the voices of and (when suppression did not work) prosecuted those who spoke and wrote against that order. As soon as they could, the parliamentary leaders dismantled the existing system of censorship—and replaced it with one of their own, in the Ordinance for the Regulating of Printing of 1643. Essentially, they replicated the king's system but reversed the polarities: if under Charles you couldn't speak against episcopal order, now you couldn't speak in favor of it. Milton's pamphlet was an eloquent protest against simply restoring an old tyranny, and proposed allowing a far greater liberty of speech than anything either the Royalist or the Parliamentary party had to that point entertained. To us, his denial of freedom to Catholics and blasphemers seems evidently absurd; to his fellow radical Protestants, the real absurdity was giving freedom of the press to the bishop-loving enemies of all that was godly and good. They saw, as did the Royalists before (and after) them, that freedom of printing and speaking would bring social disorder.

And it is vital to see that *they were not wrong*. A society in which the dissemination of information is controlled by the government will almost surely be more orderly than one in which information and disinformation are free; and the more complete the control, the more perfect will be the order. And these English politicians and pamphleteers who debated the place of printed material in their society knew that the last century of their own country had been repeatedly stained by violent disputes over the character of that nation and the religion it would profess. They also looked across the English Channel at a continent that had been riven by wars for three decades. The prospect of social disorder was not *theoretical* for them. The question they faced was one, not of good versus evil, but of *competing goods*. If we look at Milton's argument for unlicensed printing and can see only the ways in which it doesn't go far enough, without understanding why so many people who were on his side in the English Civil War thought it went considerably too far, we will not learn the lessons that history, with its "partially completed discrimination," offered us. And we will therefore lack the personal density we need to discern that the political disputes of our own moment likewise tend to concern, not good versus evil, but competing goods.

What Milton and the American Founders have in common is this: they were early and vigorous proponents of the very ideas that would later be used to denounce them. They opened a door that they chose not to walk through— but they opened it. As the English historian C. V. Wedgwood wrote in the introduction to her great history of the English Civil War, "The highest ideals put forth in this generation of conflict were noble; the men who fought or worked for them were less noble than the ideals, for the best of men do not consistently live on the highest plane of virtue, and most men live far below it." One of the traits that makes Wedgwood a truly great historian is the cold-eyed clarity with which she sees these universal deficiencies. She is never surprised by them and therefore never prone to exaggerate them. ("A cynical view of human frailty," she wrote, "is no help to the historian.") In many ways, this is the human predicament: We are all inconstant and changeable, we all shy away from the full implications of our best and strongest ideas. Why should Washington and Jefferson and Milton have been any different? We should not be surprised that they failed to live up to their ideals; we should, I think, be surprised that in their time and place they upheld such ideals at all. They pushed the world a little closer to freedom and justice. Of how many of us can that be said?

To shrug at such defects may seem to be a shameful indifference, but is potentially very useful. If we understand that this pervasive inconsistency, this inability to transcend the interests of people who look or act or believe just like us, is universal, then perhaps—just perhaps—we will be less likely to believe that *we* are immune to it. We will perceive that nothing exempts us from the same temptations and the same frailty. And perhaps, knowing that, we will be more inclined to forgive such frailty in others, just as we (most of us anyway) forgive ourselves. As has often been said, if we wonder how it's possible to, as Christians say, "hate the sin and love the sinner," it's easy: we do it to ourselves every day.

Let me offer in this context a kind of parable.

In *Tristes Tropiques*, the brilliant and unclassifiable memoir by the anthropologist Claude Lévi-Strauss, there's an account of his visit to rum distilleries in the Caribbean. In Martinique, he says he "visited rustic and neglected rum-distilleries where the equipment and the methods used had not changed since the eighteenth century." By contrast, the distilleries in Puerto Rico were thoroughly modern, with "white enamel tanks and chromium piping." The result, he explains, was that "the various kinds of Martinique rum, as I tasted them in front of ancient wooden vats thickly encrusted with waste matter, were mellow and scented, whereas those of Puerto Rico are coarse and harsh." This contrast suggested to Lévi-Strauss a more general lesson, which he names "the paradox of civilization":

> its charms are due essentially to the various residues it carries along with it, although this does not absolve us of the obligation to purify the stream. We are right to be rational and to try to increase our production and so keep manufacturing costs down. But we are also right to cherish those very imperfections we are endeavouring to eliminate. Social life consists in destroying that which gives it its savour.

Something like this, it seems to me, is the fate of all social improvements, as much as we hate to admit it——and we do. Nothing is more intrinsic to human nature than the desire to believe that benefits can and do come without costs, that we can fix certain problems without introducing new ones. We certainly don't want to admit that to those who would oppose productive change, lest we give them leverage to argue that the change shouldn't have been made at all.*

I grew up in Birmingham, Alabama, during the most intense days of the civil rights movement, days of rage and heroism, and in a family that was badly wounded by alcoholism and violence. Through most of my childhood my father was in prison, and my mother worked long hours to keep us financially afloat; my world was narrow and limited and showed no signs of broadening. I am therefore enormously grateful for a social order that allowed me economic and professional mobility, that showed me open doors and encouraged me to go through them. But I would be lying to you and deceiving myself if I denied that that mobility came with costs. I have not had the intimacy with family that my parents and grandparents had; I have not known *lifelong* friendships. When I say this I do not wish my life to be different, but it is good for me to face what I

---

*In his essay "The Prevention of Literature," George Orwell describes the attitude of political partisans to the discovery that some document has been forged by people who share their politics: "The argument that to tell the truth would be 'inopportune' or would 'play into the hands of' somebody or other is felt to be unanswerable, and few people are bothered by the prospect of the lies which they condone getting out of the newspapers and into the history books."

have missed, if for no other reason than to help me find appropriate compensations and consolations.

What is true for me on a personal level is, I believe, true for all of us in one way or another, and true *culturally*. Our culture has made certain decisions on our behalf, decisions we individuals have participated in with varying degrees of willingness, and even when we fully endorse those decisions we should not, we must not, be afraid to count the costs—to notice the ways in which the rum we make lacks the savor of that made in the old, abandoned ways, even when we affirm that abandonment. For, again, only when we do so may we seek the proper compensations and consolations for what we have left behind.

If it is foolish to think that we can carry with us all the good things from the past—from our personal past or that of our culture—while leaving behind all the unwanted baggage, it is a counsel of despair and, I think, another kind of foolishness to think that if we leave behind the errors and miseries of the past, we must also leave behind everything that gave that world its savor. Wisdom lies in discernment, and utopianism and nostalgia alike are ways of abandoning discernment.

4.

THE PAST WITHOUT
DIFFERENCE

~~~━━━◁◁▭▷▷━━━~~~

Who would be the opposite of these presentist people I have been decrying, these people whose temporal bandwidth has narrowed to the instant? Who is matter to their antimatter? I might nominate Heinrich Schliemann, the nineteenth-century German businessman who transformed himself into an archaeologist and is often described as "the discoverer of Troy."

Schliemann was obsessed with everything Greek. He divorced his wife in order to marry a Greek woman, and "baptized" his children—whom he named Andromache, Troy, and Agamemnon—by holding a copy of the *Iliad* over their heads and reciting lines from it. At one point in his excavations he discovered a great golden mask and declared, "I have looked into the face of Agamemnon." As it turned out, the mask didn't belong to Agamemnon, but Schliemann really did believe that he had gazed upon the king after whom he named his own son. He believed that he had erased the distance between his world and the world of archaic Greece that he so profoundly loved.

But as much as sheer presentism, an outlook like Schliemann's is also a diminishment of temporal bandwidth. The way that you expand your Now is not by treating the distant past as though it were present; rather, your task is to see it in its difference as well as in its likeness to your own moment. You can't close that distance by naming your son after an ancient king.

Schliemann's fascination with and love of all things Greek sometimes led him astray, disabling rather than enabling his understanding. For no one who had read the *Iliad* with any real care would name his son Agamemnon. Agamemnon was a terrible king who made one catastrophic error after another, who survived the war largely by accident—in part by claiming the prerogative of kings to stay out of the line of fire—and stumbled his long way home only to be murdered by his wife, apparently not having anticipated that she would be unhappy with him for having sacrificed their daughter to the gods. This is someone whose name you'd want to give to your child? Schliemann's idea of "ancient Greekness" made him blind to some vital considerations.

Schliemann may be an extreme case, though what makes him extreme is his use in what most of us would call a "secular" context of an approach to the past that we typically associate with religions—*bookish* religions, anyway. A common assumption made by Jews and Christians and Muslims is that their sacred texts can speak to them more or less directly across the centuries. (The situation is rather different for Buddhism, Hinduism, and Taoism, where sacred texts don't play the same governing role.) Indeed, the ability to transcend temporal and cultural distance is one of the primary traits that makes a sacred text sacred.

In 1942, when W. H. Auden was writing his "Christmas Oratorio," *For the Time Being*, he sent a copy to his father, and was rather surprised to discover that his father was puzzled and frustrated by the poem. The problem for Dr. Auden—a retired physician and a widely read man— was the way the poem blurred the lines between the ancient world and our own. For instance, in a section of the poem narrated by Herod the Great, the Judaean king makes reference to bookshops and trapeze artists.

The younger Auden replied that this approach is not new with him: "until the 18th Cent. it was always done, in the Mystery Plays for instance or any Italian paintings." And this is correct. In the mystery plays of medieval England— which reenacted stories from the Bible—the biblical characters talked, acted, and dressed like ordinary Englishmen. In many Renaissance paintings, biblical figures are dressed like people of the painter's time and are placed in obviously European, rather than Palestinian, landscapes. Auden agrees that taking up the same method in the twentieth century is risky: "If a return to the older method now seems startling it is partly because of the acceleration in the rate of historical change due to industrialization—there is a far greater difference between the accidents of life in 1600 AD and in 1942 than between those of 30 AD and 1600." At any time and place, a biblical character dressed like a Renaissance courtier is significantly less jarring than one wearing a business suit and lace-up oxfords.

For the poet, his apparently unhistorical approach arises from the fact that he's writing about the *biblical* story: "the historical fact that the shepherds were *shepherds* is religiously accidental—the religious fact is that they were the poor and humble of this world for whom at this moment the historical expression is the city-proletariat, and so on with all the other figures." For Auden, if Christianity is always and everywhere true, then you *have* to find a way to translate the Bible's concerns into the experience of your own day. At all costs Auden wants to avoid costume drama, the kind of thing that the historian C. V. Wedgwood is talking about when she comments that "it was a common romantic vice to encourage a purely theatrical view of the past, as though history were an opera house inhabited by puppets striking noble attitudes preferable in picturesque settings, and quite removed from the ordinary embarrassments and distresses of mortal life." Better an anachronistic business suit than *that*.

The kind of reading, that kind of encounter with the words of the past, which religions based on historical texts demand is a special case, and one that I won't be dealing with in the rest of this book. I pause to describe it because it has long been important to many of the world's cultures, and also because it calls our attention to one of the things that makes Schliemann so unusual: he reads secular history *as* a sacred text. Which, I think it's fair to say, is not a great idea.

But you don't have to be a Schliemann in order to

believe that the past contains treasures that we can unearth—and unearth in the cause of increasing our own personal density. One of the things you learn from studying the past is how our ancestors conceived of their own past. For the most part they did not have the same kind of historical consciousness that we have—the kind in which calling something "medieval" is meant to be, and is often received as, a one-word refutation. People who do not carry around that particular sense of difference and distance from the past do not have the same reactions, the same concerns, that Dr. Auden had.

Throughout most of the past two thousand years or so in the West, a common belief held that a person could best navigate the challenges of life by taking his or her bearings from famous figures from the past. Again, I do not speak here of the religious sensibility that looks back to Jesus or Abraham or Lao-tzu or the Buddha, but rather of the more secular sensibility that sees major actors on the world's stage as *exemplary* for us. This was true whether those figures were virtuous or vicious, because one could learn what not to do from studying the past as well as one could learn what courses were rightly pursued.

When Niccolò Machiavelli was exiled from his native Florence and forced to live in the countryside among rubes and rednecks, he admitted that he was prone to get into pointless arguments with said rubes and rednecks, but at the end of the day he could do this:

> When evening has come, I return to my house and go into my study. At the door I take off my clothes of

the day, covered with mud and mire, and I put on my regal and courtly garments; and decently reclothed, I enter the ancient courts of ancient men, where, received by them lovingly, I feed on the food that alone is mine and that I was born for. There I am not ashamed to speak with them and to ask them the reason for their actions; and they in their humanity reply to me. And for the space of four hours I feel no boredom, I forget every pain, I do not fear poverty, death does not frighten me.

Machiavelli experienced his study as a kind of time machine—recall here Brian Morton's idea that in reading books we travel to the past—but when he receives the company of the Greats he feels no temporal distinction from them. They speak to him "in their humanity," a humanity that cheerfully disregards boundaries of time and space.

Machiavelli here engages chiefly with the thinkers of the past—but what about history's actors, the great political and military figures who bestrode their own times like giants? Certainly as he wrote *The Prince*, the manual of political action he offered to Lorenzo de' Medici in hopes of being restored to influence in Florence, he saw princes and kings and warriors of the past as offering examples for modern rulers to learn from—but, and this has always been the most controversial element of *The Prince*, they are merely examples of success and failure, not virtue and vice. In offering his advice to Lorenzo, Machiavelli was consciously setting himself apart from a long-standing tradition, one that made the leaders of the past somehow contemporary with later readers, and object lessons for them. The person who did more than any other to create this tradition was the Greek-speaking Roman historian Plutarch, who lived from around 46 CE to around 120 CE, and who wrote his series of lives of Greek and Roman statesmen and other notables explicitly in order to provide examples, mirrors in which people could perceive their own virtues and vices.

Plutarch was born in the village of Chaeronea, in Boeotia, and though he spent some time in Athens, he lived in Chaeronea for most of his life. (He once commented that he stayed there in order to prevent the small town from becoming even smaller.) Plutarch thought that one could live a wise and fulfilling life anywhere, and that was possible in part because of books—books that connect us to the Great. He wrote a number of *Moralia*—moral essays, essays that offered sage advice for good living—but he came to feel that mere precepts were inadequate for communicating to people the best way to live. We need examples of virtue and vice in action in order to see their outlines clearly, and the lives of the Great wrote their examples of virtue and vice in very large letters that all could clearly read. Thus he emphasized that his lives were biographies, not histories, which did not mean that they were inaccurate but rather than he sought primarily to include evidence of character, which might come from trivial events in a person's life. So he warned his readers that if they wanted detailed accounts of Alexander the Great's military conquests they should look elsewhere; but if they wanted to understand the unique combination of personal traits that made Alexander who he so memorably was, for good and for ill, Plutarch's Life of Alexander is just the thing.

In an introduction to one of his Lives he wrote,

> Although I originally took up the writing of Lives for others, I find that the task has grown on me and I continue with it for my own sake too, in the sense that I treat the narrative as a kind of mirror and try to find a way to arrange my life and assimilate it to the virtues of my subjects. The experience is like nothing so much as spending time in their company and living with them: I receive and welcome each of them in turn as my guest, so to speak, observe "his stature and his qualities," and choose from his achievements those which it is particularly important and valuable for me to know. "And oh, what greater delight could one find than this?" And could one find a more effective means of moral improvement either?

Notice how closely this resembles Machiavelli, but not the author of *The Prince*; rather, the man who lived in the country and spoke with the ancients in his library. (Surely *that* Machiavelli was taking his bearings from Horace, with whom we began this book, as he sought to "interrogate the writings of the wise.") Machievelli: "There I am not ashamed to speak with them and to ask them the reason for their actions; and they in their humanity reply to me." Plutarch: "I receive and welcome each of them in turn as my guest, so to speak, observe 'his stature and his qualities,' and choose from his achievements those which it is particularly important and valuable for me to know." It's the same ap-

proach, but Machiavelli sought communion with philosophers and poets, Plutarch with warriors and emperors.
The great figures of the past, then, provide sustenance for
those who seek the contemplative life *and* the active.

Plutarch's way of appropriating and drawing on the experiences of the great political and military figures of
Greece and Rome proved to be profoundly influential for
many centuries. It was intrinsically comparative—each life
of a Greek figure was paired with the closest Roman coun-
terpart, for instance Alexander with Julius Caesar—and
therefore encouraged further comparison with the lives
of the political figures of one's own era. His model was one
that the whole educational system of western Europe em-
braced for a very long time. Thanks to Plutarch it not only
seemed natural to George Washington to perceive himself
as a modern analogue of Cincinnatus—the great general
who saved the Roman Republic and then retired to his
farm—but it was equally natural to everyone else who
knew Washington or merely observed him to assess him in
comparison to the character of Cincinnatus. (As it happens, Plutarch did not write a life of Cincinnatus—a major
oversight, if you ask me—but he established the pattern by
which Washington and his contemporaries thought about
the relationship between the present and the past.)

In a wonderfully illuminating book, *Cincinnatus: George
Washington and the Enlightenment*, Garry Wills tells the
story of a conversation that took place during the Revolutionary War between England's King George III and his
court painter, the Pennsylvania-born Benjamin West. The

king asked West what he thought General Washington would do if he happened to defeat the British, and West replied that he would simply return to his plantation at Mount Vernon. George replied that if Washington did that he would be the greatest man who ever lived. Cincinnatus is never mentioned in the conversation; he did not have to be mentioned. Both men knew that the Roman's example provided the context for the whole affair.

And by accepting the association Washington bound himself to certain standards, invited others to judge him by them, and made the same judgments upon himself. On the Lawn of the University of Virginia there is a statue of George Washington. He stands next to the *fasces*—the bundle of rods that in Republican Rome represented the authority given to what they called the *dictator*, and from which we take our word "fascist"—and his farmer's plow lies behind him. Directly across the Lawn there is another statue, of Thomas Jefferson sitting and looking intently at Washington. He is waiting to see if the general will, like Cincinnatus, set aside the *fasces* and once more take up his innocent plow.

This attitude—in which figures from the past stand forth clearly and vividly in the present, almost as though they are our contemporaries—lasted into the twentieth century. The Plutarchian frame of mind was essential to the thinking of Winston Churchill, for instance, who as a writer as well as a statesman perceived the past with an *immediacy* that seems strange to most of us today. In a speech Churchill gave in 1909, when he was still known primarily as a journalist, he said:

Someone—I forget who—has said: "Words are the only things which last forever." That is, to my mind, always a wonderful thought. The most durable structures raised in stone by the strength of man, the mightiest monuments of his power, crumble into dust, while the words spoken with fleeting breath, the passing expression of the unstable fancies of his mind, endure not as echoes of the past, not as mere archaeological curiosities or venerable relics, but with a force and life as new and strong, and sometimes far stronger than when they were first spoken, and leaping across the gulf of three thousand years, they light the world for us to-day.

From the context you can tell that Churchill was referring less to the philosophers and poets with whom Machiavelli communed in his library than to public figures or writers concerned with politics: historians like Thucydides and Livy, orators like Cicero, historians of their own deeds like Caesar.

A very similar attitude may be found in Churchill's contemporary G. K. Chesterton, who in an essay titled "On Man: Heir of All the Ages" argued that we have the whole of history available to us as our rightful inheritance, and that "the mind of man is at its largest, and especially at its broadest, when it feels the brotherhood of humanity linking it up with remote and primitive and even barbaric things." Alas, says Chesterton, "If the modern man is indeed the heir of all the ages, he is often the kind of heir who tells the family solicitor to sell the whole damned estate, lock, stock, and barrel, and give him a little ready money to throw away at the races or the nightclubs."

The reader who has come with me this far will not be surprised to learn that I nod smilingly when I read this passage, and nod more soberly and firmly when I arrive here: "Any man who is cut off from the past, and content with the future, is a man most unjustly disinherited; and all the more unjustly if he is happy in his lot, and is not permitted even to know what he has lost." I find it especially interesting that Chesterton believes that the archaic, the primitive, is still an element of our psychological and moral constitution, though it has been obscured by the addition of more recent layers. So one reason to read old books is to get in touch with those elements of our constitution that we're least likely to notice otherwise.

So yes, I find much to admire in the arguments of Churchill and Chesterton, and in the way they boldly carry the Plutarchian model of the relevance of past people and ideas into the twentieth century . . . but I am also made uneasy by these arguments. They don't go as far as Schliemann in erasing the distance between us and the people of the past, writers and actors alike, but they certainly underplay that distance. And I think this can lead first to misunderstanding the past and second to devaluing the best gifts that encounters with the past can actually bring to us.

I have argued that we can sometimes be deterred from what an old book offers by noticing where it falls short— our inclination to negative selection can blind us to the virtues of positive selection. But we can also get ourselves into something like the opposite problem—a determination to read in a sanitizing way—when faced with a text that we know is in some sense a "classic" but which offends, or seems to offend. Take, for instance, a work I mentioned earlier, Shakespeare's *The Taming of the Shrew*, in which Katharine, that rebellious and insubordinate woman, is "tamed" by Petruchio. There is absolutely no reason to believe that Shakespeare's view of their conflict differs in any way from Petruchio's. When Petruchio says of Katherine's prospective obedience to him that "peace it bodes, and love and quiet life, / An awful [that is, awe-inspiring] rule and right supremacy, / And, to be short, what's not that's sweet and happy?" he makes an argument very similar to ones made by some quite admirable characters in Shakespeare's other plays. (See, for instance, the famous speech in praise of "degree"—social hierarchy—made by Ulysses in *Troilus and Cressida*.)

And yet it has been a very long time, I wager, since any reputable theater company put on the play in this spirit. Every director who wants to keep his or her job finds a way to undermine Petruchio's patriarchal assurance, most often by making sure that Katherine follows up her late subservient speech—"Such duty as the subject owes the prince, / Even such a woman oweth to her husband"— with broad winks to the audience or to the other women onstage. Long ago C. S. Lewis wrote that Petruchio's words "are very startling to a modern audience; but those who cannot face such startling should not read old books." This is harsh, I think—there are good reasons why women who know that the patriarchal order has scarcely been demolished might prefer not to sit and watch a celebration of it—but there *is* something a little odd, and not satisfactory, about trying to *combine* a disinclination to be "startled," at least in that way, with an appreciation for "the classics." Maybe there's something to be said for those who just refuse to read or watch such stuff: at least that refusal acknowledges that you can't simply reshape "startling" texts in your own image. Surely we have lost something vital when we have lost the power to be startled, even offended, by the voices from the past. To say "This text offends me, I will read no further" may be shortsighted; but to read a "great book" from the past with such reverence that you can't see where its views are wrong, or even where they differ from your own, is no better. Indeed, in foreclosing the possibility of real challenge it is worse.

Not all works from the past are classics, and there are often good reasons to read old books that don't merit that designation, but there's an essay on the classics by the Italian novelist Italo Calvino that I think helps to clarify the tension between likeness and difference that I have been trying to call attention to. Calvino begins by emphasizing the "affinities" we can experience with old books: "In a classic we sometimes discover something we have always known (or thought we knew), but without knowing that this author said it first, or at least is associated with it in a special way. And this, too, is a surprise that gives a lot of pleasure, such as we always gain from the discovery of an origin, a relationship, an affinity."

But Calvino also talks about "*your* classics," books that take on classic status for a particular reader: "*Your* classic author is the one you cannot feel indifferent to, who helps you to define yourself in relation to him, *even in dispute with him*" (that second emphasis mine). That is, a book becomes a classic for you in part because of its power to compel you to hear something that you not only hadn't thought but might not believe, or might not want to believe. In this sense a book can become very much like a friend: When we enter into a conversation with a friend, do we want that person merely to nod approvingly at everything we say? Of course not: in many cases we want sympathy and agreement, to be sure, but a friend who offered *only* that would be no friend at all. When we speak our thought, we want more than agreement, we want *addition*: we want our friend to develop that thought, or to push back at it, if ever so gently. We want to get further along in our understanding of ourselves and our world than we were when we first spoke, and that cannot happen through mere affirmation. Perhaps the poet William Blake had something like this in mind when he wrote "Opposition is true friendship." The work that is classic for me is the one that can give me, among other things, *that* kind of opposition.

And when that happens, the conversation I am having with that book comes to the forefront of my consciousness. Calvino says something very shrewd and very subtle about this: "A classic is something that tends to relegate the concerns of the moment to the status of background noise, but at the same time this background noise is something we cannot do without." Both halves of this sentence are essential. The reader who instantly translates the subject or story of a book into present-day terms often is not having a genuine encounter with the book at all. (In Dickens's

David Copperfield Mister Dick keeps trying to write a book only to find that King Charles's head—the debodied head of the executed English King Charles I—keeps inexplicably making its way into the narrative. A certain president's head keeps doing that in the thoughts of many of my fellow Americans.) But that the book I am reading is *somehow* connected to my life is an essential ambience to reading, "something we cannot do without."

A few years ago the critic Daniel Mendelsohn wrote a beautiful essay on reading and teaching Virgil's *Aeneid*, which most college students, if my thirty years of experience are anything to go by, find far less compelling than the earlier epics of Homer. Mendelsohn describes both the centrality of the *Aeneid* to the Western imagination and the various impediments to getting excited about it. There are several, but Mendelsohn thinks that at our moment the "the biggest problem by far for modern audiences" is what the poem is fundamentally *about*. "Today, the themes that made the epic required reading for generations of emperors and generals, and for the clerics and teachers who groomed them—the inevitability of imperial dominance, the responsibilities of authoritarian rule, the importance of duty and self-abnegation in the service of the state—are proving to be an embarrassment."

It's fascinating to read how Mendelsohn—who is one of the shrewdest literary critics now writing—navigates these difficulties. Does Virgil support empire, or critique it? And if the former, can we modern democrats still like him? Or must we be alienated from this work that many of our ancestors felt so immediately the power of? Without offering a definitive answer to these questions, Mendelsohn describes the time in his life "when, I like to think, I finally began to understand the *Aeneid*." And he does this by taking Calvino's "background noise" of our own moment and bringing it to the foreground:

> Months later, when I was back home teaching Greek and Roman classics again, it occurred to me that the difficulties we have with Aeneas and his epic cease to be difficulties once you think of him not as a hero but as a type we're all too familiar with: a survivor, a person so fractured by the horrors of the past that he can hold himself together only by an unnatural effort of will, someone who has so little of his history left that the only thing that gets him through the present is a numbed sense of duty to a barely discernible future that can justify every kind of deprivation. It would be hard to think of a more modern figure.

I think this is a connection to the present that's *earned*—which is not always the case in essays of this type. For instance, the English writer Philip Hoare recently commended *Moby-Dick* in an essay for *The Guardian* of London in which he praises the book for being "relevant" to our climate crisis, for being a "very queer book," for being "genuinely subversive"—for, in general, being all the things that *Guardian* readers already approve of. Hoare clearly thinks that this approach is the only way to generate interest in an old book. But if *Moby-Dick* simply reaffirms our current state of opinion, why bother to read it at all?

Daniel Mendelsohn, by contrast, didn't immediately leap

to a modern "application" of the *Aeneid*—like the person (we all know the type) whose response to everyone else's pain is to be reminded of his own, which he then wants to narrate at length—but rather wrestled with the poem *on its own terms* for years before finally realizing that the experiences of our time actually bring to light something real and true about this great poem that would have been invisible to those among our ancestors who most warmly venerated it.

One more illustration may serve to clarify and intensify the point that I have been making. Tom Stoppard's play *The Invention of Love* (1997) begins with the English poet and classical scholar A. E. Housman, "aged seventy-seven and getting no older" because he's dead, being transported across the Styx by Charon, the boatman of the land of Hades. And then when he reaches the other side of the river he finds . . . himself, a fresh-faced Oxford undergraduate. And the two Housmans talk, mainly about Roman writers.

At one point the elder Housman (here called AEH) fires off an impromptu lecture on the dangers of simply assuming that we understand the writers of the distant past:

> There are always poetical people ready to protest that a corrupt line is exquisite. Exquisite to whom? The Romans were foreigners writing for foreigners two millenniums ago; and for people whose gods we find quaint, whose savagery we abominate, whose private habits we don't like to talk about, but whose idea of what is exquisite is, we flatter ourselves, mysteriously identical with ours.

At this moment the young Houseman, unable to bear this discourse an instant longer, bursts out: "But it *is*, isn't it? We catch our breath at the places where the breath was always caught." In his enthusiasm, he starts to quote examples from love poems and letters of phrases that have caught his breath, and then, equally suddenly, is seized by embarrassment and self-consciousness and stops: "Oh, forgive me, I . . ."

To which the elderly, or rather the *dead*, AEH quietly replies: "No need, we're never too old to learn." Young Housman starts up again instantly, but we should pause here for one of the loveliest moments in modern drama. AEH, long accustomed to his own authority—he was the greatest classical scholar of his time, and devastatingly fierce in his denunciations of what he believed to be the shortcomings of almost all his peers—realizes that for all his massive learning he has forgotten something of great import: That even granted the differences in belief and habit that separate us from the Romans, we can and *do* read their poems and find that "we catch our breath at the places where the breath was always caught." He had once known it, but then he forgot.

What makes this moment so beautiful, I think, is that both AEH and Housman are right. AEH rightly understands the dangers of assuming an easy and immediate kinship with the past—he knows better than to become Schliemann, or even the young Churchill—and that any *genuine* kinship with our ancestors must be earned through hard mental work. But if what the young Housman says were not true, there would scarcely be any reason to read these works at all.

I think this necessary tension is lost both by those who once saw education as the inculcation of reverence for the past *and* their successors who have redefined education so that it's wholly presentist or forward-looking. The person who did more than anyone else to shift the energies of educators from the model that Churchill and Chesterton loved to the one most of us today have experienced is the American philosopher John Dewey, but if you look at Dewey's understanding of what education is, you can see the possibility for a sensitive encounter with the past. In a book of a hundred years ago, Dewey wrote, "We thus reach a technical definition of education: It is that reconstruction or reorganization of experience which adds to the meaning of experience, and which increases ability to direct the course of subsequent experience." Properly understood, Dewey's formulation suggests continuity as well as innovation: taking what we have inherited and, rather than discarding it, reorganizing and reconstructing it—a task that can be performed intelligently only if we sift the past for its wisdom and its wickedness, its perception and its foolishness. And this is a task not merely for scholars but for us all.

When I was in high school, we didn't read any ancient writers in my classes. We read some Hawthorne and Melville and Washington Irving, and George Eliot's *Silas Marner*, and *A Tale of Two Cities* and *Great Expectations*, and then, reaching into "the dark backward and abysm of time," a Shakespeare play each year, though not the one that phrase comes from (*The Tempest*). I don't recall anyone ever explaining to me why we were reading these things; certainly there was no reflection on the relative ages of the works, or whether it might matter that George Eliot was separated from her contemporaries Hawthorne and Melville by an ocean. If my memory doesn't deceive me, the first time a figure from the past spoke to me directly and gave me a sense of instant kinship across the centuries was when I discovered this line by Chaucer: "The lyf so short, the craft so longe to lerne." Why that should have been so moving to me when I was so young and had as yet no "craft" at all, I cannot tell.

When I got to university I learned much more about literature and history, but the kind of sifting of the words of the past I've described here was something I learned not from my professors, who never recommended as personal an appropriation as I have been advocating throughout this book, but in my private reading. In an earlier book I recommended reading "upstream" from our favorite novels, and that's just what I did. I took a couple of classes in medieval literature but I came to adore that anonymous masterpiece *Sir Gawain and the Green Knight* because I knew Tolkien had loved it. "What we have loved, / Others will love, and we will teach them how," wrote Wordsworth, and the ones who taught me how were primarily writers. I loved their stories, so I was prepared to love the stories they loved. From my teachers I learned to be like AEH, measured, distanced, analytical; from my favorite writers I learned to be like young Housman, full of enthusiasm and striving for connection. Both lessons were lastingly

valuable, but my writer-teachers have made a greater difference to my life, and it is what I have learned from them
that I have poured into this book.

Breaking bread with the dead is not a scholarly task to
be completed but a permanent banquet, to which all who
hunger are invited.

5

THE AUTHENTIC KERNEL

The kind of "positive selection" that I have recommended—it's easy to talk about, isn't it?

For many years I taught literary theory to undergraduates—I will gladly accept your sympathy in the currency of chocolate—and for most of those years I included in my unit on feminist criticism an essay by a scholar named Patrocinio Schweickart called "Reading Ourselves: Toward a Feminist Theory of Reading." I taught the essay every year because I love it, and I love it because of how honestly and intelligently Schweickart faces a common and serious problem.

Imagine that you are a deeply committed feminist. (You may not need to imagine!) You see with crystal clarity the ramifying effects of the patriarchy throughout history, woven through the whole fabric of human life. You have been trained to pay exceptionally close attention to such phenomena, even when they are present in subtle and silent ways. Imagine then that you pick up a book, a Victorian novel, say—a novel by a man. You read the book, and

you discover that it indeed manifests at every turn com-
plicity in patriarchal ideology. You also discover . . . that it
moves you. It touches you. You are caught up in its story,
and you care about its characters.

What do you do *now*?

You might do several things. You might set the book
down before it affects you any further. Schweickart does not
recommend this. You might, alternatively, become more
deeply drawn into in the thought-world of the book and increasingly assume its masculine point of view—Schweickart
calls this being "immasculated," being immersed in mascu-
linity, and she does not recommend this either.

Instead, she suggests, you should look for what she calls
a "utopian moment"—a moment when something deeply
and beautifully human emerges from that swamp of patriarchal ideology. Another phrase she uses for this is the "authentic kernel," something perhaps hidden deep inside the
book that speaks to you, that articulates an experience you
can share. From this point on you read in a *double* fashion.
You don't silence the part of you that sees the problems
with the book, its errors, its moral malformations; neither
do you silence the part of you that responds so warmly to
that "utopian moment."

Oddly enough, this creative doubleness may be easier
for *writers* than for readers. Sometimes when a story both
entrances and offends you, you'd love to alter it or add to it
in ways that redress its imbalances. If you're a writer, you
can do this. This is, importantly I think, one of the chief
prompts for fan fiction, which, despite its name, doesn't

just celebrate the works it draws on: sometimes it extends, sometimes it even corrects them.

Imagine, now, that you are a woman reading a story written by a man, and that story contains as a pivotal character a woman—but that woman is not allowed to speak. It is easy to think of an example: indeed, one of the works we discussed in the previous chapter readily provides one. That work is the *Aeneid*.

In the *Aeneid*, a young woman named Lavinia is the daughter of King Latinus of Latium, in Italy. Two rivals compete for her hand: Turnus, king of the Rutuli, and Aeneas, a wanderer, an exile from fallen Troy. The gods, in their inscrutable counsel, have determined that Lavinia shall marry Aeneas and inaugurate the line of the Romans-to-be; and so, therefore, it befalls. Virgil has conjured this princess out of legend into literary being, has surrounded her with beautiful words, has described the loveliness of her virginal blushes.* But her blushes are her only speech.

Earlier I spoke of giving voice to the dead with the blood of our attention. An idea very like this animates Ursula K. Le Guin's superb novel titled simply *Lavinia*. Le Guin's Lavinia knows that she has been called forth by Virgil's language and responds to this with a curious mixture

---

*"*Accepit vocem lacrimis Lavinia matris / flagrantis perfusa genas, cui plurimus ignem / subiecit rubor et calefacta per ora cucurrit*"—or, as David Ferry's translation has it,

Lavinia, hearing these words of her mother, wept,
And her beautiful face, bathed in her tears, was like,
In its alternate blushing and pallor a garden where
There are lilies, white, and crimson roses, or like
An Indian ivory painted with blood-red dyes. . . .

of gratitude and discontent. "No doubt I will eventually fade away and be lost in oblivion, as I would have done long ago if the poet hadn't summoned me into existence." But "the splendid, vivid words I've lived in for centuries" are insufficient. "Once at least I must break out and speak. He didn't let me say a word. I have to take the word from him. He gave me a long life but a small one." And so, through Ursula K. Le Guin, Lavinia uses her own words to shape for herself a more spacious being.

Le Guin does not use her story to provide a revisionist history of Virgil's poem. She could, perhaps, have recast Aeneas as a masterful colonialist, a figure out of the Patriarchy Rulebook. She chooses not to. Her Aeneas, like that of Virgil, is reluctantly warlike, quiet when not compelled to speak, always tinged with melancholy. He loves Lavinia, and she loves him in return. Insofar as Le Guin "revises," she does so in this way: her novel is not Aeneas's story. He rarely speaks and we never are ushered into his mind, because it is not *his* mind that Le Guin wishes to illuminate, it is Lavinia's. The novel's task is to let this silent girl, who ended up living a long life, to have her voice. "Once at least I must break out and speak." And the story she tells for herself is a powerful one.

For a more ideologically revisionist example of this revisiting of the "classics," we might consider Jean Rhys's novel *Wide Sargasso Sea* (1966). Rhys had read Charlotte Brontë's *Jane Eyre*, by any measure one of the greatest of English novels, and surely she had been moved by the tale of poor Jane, who navigated her way so uncertainly through an unsympathetic world, who ended up falling in love with her employer, Mr. Rochester—a man who could not marry her (though he tried) because he was already married, to an insane women whom he kept confined in rooms on the third floor of his country house.

For Rhys, the most interesting thing about this mad lady was her origin: she was a Creole, born and raised in Jamaica as Bertha Antoinetta Mason. Rhys herself was not a Creole, but had been born on the island of Dominica, and had come to England when she was sixteen; that connection, it seems, led her to think about this fictional woman. What had driven her to madness? When she was a young beauty in Jamaica, what had been her hopes and dreams? We know her story as the rich Englishman Rochester would tell it, and Rochester's young new wife—but how would Bertha Antoinetta herself tell it? From this question *Wide Sargasso Sea* arose.

Jane Eyre was written by a woman; but a woman to some degree confined by her upbringing in West Yorkshire, an environment in which words like "Jamaica" and "Dominica" were little more *than* words; to her Bertha Antoinetta was silent, exotic—perhaps silent *because* exotic. Rhys, to whom the Caribbean was home, wanted to give voice to the woman she calls Antoinetta.

Reader, you may not also be a writer. But I provide these examples anyway because I think they are instructive to us all. What drove Le Guin and Rhys to write their powerful novels was not *merely* frustration, but rather frustration mixed with admiration and even love. The *Aeneid* and *Jane Eyre* are truly great works of literary art—*that is what makes them worth responding to.* Lesser works with the same flaws, the same blind spots, could simply be set aside. These books could not be so dismissed.

I want to argue that the response Le Guin and Rhys make to their predecessors in storytelling is best described as *generous*. Kathleen Fitzpatrick has recently written a book that's focused on the renewal of academic life but has much broader relevance. It's called *Generous Thinking*, and generosity is a vital concept that we need to appropriate. Generosity, for Fitzpatrick, is both habit and deed, but above all an *ongoing disposition*—"generosity as an enduring habit of mind, a conversational practice"—and (this is essential) a disposition that arises from a kind of hope. You are generous toward someone else—you give them more of your attention than you may at certain moments feel that they deserve—because you hope that something good will come of it. At the very least you hope for an expansion of your own understanding—and in the terms I've been using throughout this book, an accumulation of personal density.

In an age such as ours focused on justice, it can be hard to keep our eyes on this particular prize. It is easy for even the most genuine passion for justice to assume a punitive aspect: we don't like to see people getting away with bad behavior. We want them to get what they deserve, and *not* to get what they *don't* deserve. This attitude is more than understandable, but it can be hard to see whether it's compatible with generosity. Think back to the young man Brian Morton knew who didn't want Edith Wharton's *House of Mirth* in his own house. Much of this revulsion, as I commented earlier, arises from a sense of defilement, but at least a part of it is also not wanting for Wharton the anti-Semite to get more respect and admiration than she deserves.

But here's one of the most important traits of authors of old books: they're dead. You can neither punish them nor reward them. They should not factor into your calculus of reward. (It's a little more complicated when you're dealing with living people, of course, but this book doesn't deal in living people. Please go to Kathleen Fitzpatrick's book for that.) You are free to extend generosity to them because it benefits *you*. Go ahead and be selfish: think only of your own personal density. That is reason enough to be generous.

Because Rhys and Le Guin extended generosity to those books of the past—because they, at the same time that they offered critique, also sought that "utopian moment," that "authentic kernel" of humanity—they were able to produce powerful and moving responses to those books, responses that complicate and enrich *our* experiences of those books too. You might even say that they make "generative odd-kin"—connecting those earlier writers not only to themselves but also to us. Generosity can be viral.

But note that generosity is not simply assuming the best of some writer or text from the past. It is, rather, a kind of struggle: taking the past seriously enough to argue with it. Recall Calvino: "*Your* classic author is the one you cannot feel indifferent to, who helps you to define yourself in relation to him, even in dispute with him." I think also of Jacob, in the book of Genesis, who, by the side of a stream called Jabbok, all through the night, wrestles with "a man." They grapple for hours, and then, as the sun rises, the man has had enough, but Jacob says to him, "I will not let you go until you bless me." Jacob later says that it was God he wrestled with, but that is a rather demanding attitude to take toward a deity, is it not? But note *what* Jacob demands. Indeed, to think that struggle and demand are incompatible with reverence is perhaps to misunderstand what reverence is—even what authority itself is.

In a once famous poem, Rudyard Kipling writes about "The Gods of the Copybook Headings." Long ago, young people learned cursive handwriting through the use of "copybooks," notebooks that came emblazoned, across the top of each page, with a sentence written in precisely the kind of hand that the student was supposed to master. The student's task was to copy that maxim line after line, from the top of the page to the bottom, ideally approximating the elegance of the heading ever more closely. By the time I got to school we didn't have copybooks; rather, the teacher would write on the board something like "The quick brown fox jumped over the lazy dog," and we would doggedly imitate the way she formed her letters. But in older days pedagogues thought that copybook headings provided an opportunity to teach not only penmanship but also virtue, so they would line the tops of their pages with sententious maxims of the *Poor Richard's Almanack* variety, warnings against vice or exhortations to virtue. "Good nature, like a bee, collects honey from every herb."

The theme of Kipling's poem is, more or less, "Everything I needed to know I learned from the copybook headings." They provided simple but unshakable wisdom; they put in brief, lapidary form the lessons to be learned from books like Plutarch's Lives; they reminded us again and again "That Water would certainly wet us, as Fire would certainly burn," and that "The Wages of Sin is Death." But we characteristically neglect the proper worship of the Gods of the Copybook Headings because we prefer the gentler gospel of those deities I mentioned earlier: the Gods of the Market Place. But those gentler Gods repeatedly deceived us—Kipling is surely right about that at least—and so:

> Then the Gods of the Market tumbled, and their
>   smooth-tongued wizards withdrew
> And the hearts of the meanest were humbled and
>   began to believe it was true
> That All is not Gold that Glitters, and Two and Two
>   make Four
> And the Gods of the Copybook Headings limped up
>   to explain it once more.*

For Kipling the great thing about the Gods of the Copybook Headings is that their wisdom is eternal: "They never altered their pace, / Being neither cloud nor wind-borne like the Gods of the Market Place." But—again admitting the shrewdness of the description of those Market Place deities—is it really the case that ancient wisdom in maxim form supplies all our needs? If human nature never changes, human circumstances do, so even if the copybook headings

---

*This stanza is especially good: "With the Hopes that our World is built on they were utterly out of touch, / They denied that the Moon was Stilton; they denied she was even Dutch; / They denied that Wishes were Horses; they denied that a Pig had Wings; / So we worshipped the Gods of the Market Who promised these beautiful things."

are both inerrant and complete, we must learn to *apply* them to our current challenges. And that requires something other and more than obedient copying.

In brief, it requires us to be like Jacob, who wrestled with a mighty figure by the Jabbok not in order to defeat or destroy him, but with a strange generosity, an eager and earnest belief that his opponent had something of great value in his possession, and that he could give it to Jacob. *I will not let you go until you bless me.*

6.

THE BOY IN THE LIBRARY

———

Peter Abrahams was born in Vrededorp, a suburb of Johannesburg, South Africa, in 1919. His family was poor, and his education consequently spotty. (In the tripartite system of apartheid South Africa, Abrahams was neither white nor black, but colored. However, he had skin dark enough to make people *think* that he was black, which cost him no end of trouble.) By the time he was ten years old, he had acquired, with considerable difficulty, three books. One was a famous anthology of British poetry called *Palgrave's Golden Treasury*; a second was Charles and Mary Lamb's *Tales from Shakespeare*; the third was an Everyman edition of the poems of John Keats. These books meant the world to Abrahams. They showed him beauty and possibility and hope.

But again, his family was poor, and they needed him to work. School was a luxury they could not afford. So he found himself on the streets of Johannesburg carrying groceries and doing other menial tasks for white women for just pennies a day. His love of poetry faded, as did his hope for a better life than the one he had: all his energy was taken up by the challenges of collecting those pennies.

And then one day he was standing on a street corner in Johannesburg next to a well-dressed black man who had a newspaper tucked under his arm. As Abrahams idly scanned the headlines he attracted the curiosity of the man, who knew that this little black boy could not possibly be literate. Yet upon questioning, he discovered that the boy could indeed read. Embarrassed by his own too easy assumption, he asked Abrahams to go to a nearby place called the Bantu Men's Social Centre and ask for work there. The center had been founded just a few years earlier by an American minister named Ray E. Phillips and was already on its way to becoming a fixture in the social world of black and colored residents of Johannesburg. (Just a few years after Abrahams showed up, a young man named Nelson Mandela would become a member.)

The center took Abrahams in and gave him some work to do, and when time permitted he browsed the shelves of the center's library. There he came across a curious book. It was by a man named W. E. B. Du Bois, and it was called *The Souls of Black Folk*, and when Abrahams opened it he saw a strange and powerful sentence: "For this much all men know: despite compromise, war, struggle, the Negro is not free." As he reports in his 1954 autobiography, *Tell Freedom*, Abrahams was stunned by this clear and crisp formulation: "But why had I not thought of it myself? Now, having read the words, I knew that I had known this all along. But until now I had had no words to voice that knowledge. Du Bois's words had the impact of a revelation."

That first book lead to many others: "In the months that followed, I spent nearly all my spare time in the library of the Bantu Men's Social Centre. I read every one of the books on the shelf marked: American Negro literature. I became a nationalist, a colour nationalist, through the writings of men and women who lived a world away from me."

And yet—this is the really fascinating thing about Abrahams's story—his discovery did not abolish or even displace his love for the three books from England that had nurtured him so richly before his discovery in the Bantu Men's Social Centre Library. Instead, there arose in him a profound tension between the different kinds of aspirations presented to him by these two sets of books. "My mind was divided," he wrote. "The call of America's limitless opportunities was strong. The call of Harlem, Negro colleges, and of the 'new Negro' writers, was compelling. But Charles Lamb, John Keats, Shelley, and the glorious host they lead made a counter call."

Another young person who would hear the call of John Keats, decades later, was the English writer Zadie Smith. When she was a teenager, around 1990, growing up as a mixed-race child in Willesden, in northwest London, and just beginning to think that she might want to write, Keats became vital for her, as a voice and an example. "I was fourteen when I heard John Keats . . . and in my mind I formed a bond with him, a bond based on class." True, "Keats was not working-class, exactly,"—though I think his early life was indeed working-class—"nor black, but in rough outline his situation seemed closer to mine than the

other writers you came across. He felt none of the entitle-
ment of, say, Virginia Woolf, or Byron, or Pope, or Evelyn
Waugh or even P. G. Wodehouse and Agatha Christie."
That Keats was an outsider with no clear path into the literary world was key to his appeal for Smith. "Keats offers
his readers the possibility of entering writing from a side
door, the one marked 'Apprentices Welcome Here.'"

Keats was a white man, Zadie Smith a mixed-race
woman. But they had much in common too: they were not
just English but also Londoners, even though Willesden
had been a country town in Keats's day. It meant a lot to
Smith to notice and lean on those connections. "The term
role model is so odious, but the truth is it's a very strong
writer indeed who gets by without a model kept somewhere in mind. I think of Keats."

Peter Abrahams almost certainly knew nothing about
Keats's upbringing. And others of his favorites he had not
even that in common with. The English language alone,
and the beauty with which those writers used it, seems to
have been the attraction. And as powerfully as the Harlem
writers spoke to Abrahams's condition, that beauty was
irresistible.

Abrahams knew that he would leave South Africa if he
could manage it. But he had to assess the "two forces that
pulled me, first this way, then that." It was clear that
"America had more to offer me as a black man. If the
American Negro was not free, he was, at least, free to give
voice to his unfreedom." And yet "England, holding out no
offer, not even the comfort of being among my own kind,
could counter that call." But how was that? "Because men

now dead had once crossed its heaths and walked its lanes, quietly, unhurriedly, and had sung with such beauty that their songs had pierced the heart of a black boy, a world away, and in another time." The enchantment arose from distance and difference.

> I decided. I would go to England one day. Perhaps I would go to America afterwards, but I would go to England first. I would go there because the dead men who called were, for me, more alive than the most vitally living.

In 1939 Abrahams made his way to London, and lived in England, writing fiction and journalism, until 1956, when he moved to Jamaica, his home for the rest of his life.

"My mind was divided." We observed a similar condition in the previous chapter, where we saw readerly minds divided between skepticism and hope, between critical incision and the quest for a "utopian moment." But this is a rather different kind of division. Whether holding his three books or a copy of *The Souls of Black Folk*, Abrahams seeks encouragement—encouragement to pursue something higher and better than a life of serving white Johannesburg women for pennies and going home at night to the slums. But as compelling as Du Bois's voice was to him—after all, his reading of "American Negro literature" *did* make him a "colour nationalist"—the voices of the dead English poets were more compelling still: "the dead men who called were, for me, more alive than the most vitally living." What they offered him was the temporal bandwidth that increased his personal density in ways he could not define but that he came to feel essential to his well-being. Perhaps at another stage of his life he would need to hear a different message, drink from a different well. But at that moment it was the English poets who commanded his allegiance. And so he made his way to England.

At the end of the eighteenth century, in Boston, Massachusetts, a man named Caleb Bingham published an anthology entitled *The Columbian Orator: Containing a Variety of Original and Selected Pieces Together with Rules, Which Are Calculated to Improve Youth and Others, in the Ornamental and Useful Art of Eloquence.* The book became enormously popular, was used in schools all over the United States, went through many revisions and new editions, and then, decades after its first publication, fell into the hands of a barely literate slave boy in Virginia, a boy we know as Frederick Douglass. In his autobiography, he describes the experience:

> I was now about twelve years old, and the thought of being a *slave for life* began to bear heavily upon my heart. Just about this time, I got hold of a book entitled "The Columbian Orator." Every opportunity I got, I used to read this book. Among much of other interesting matter, I found in it a dialogue between a master and his slave. The slave was represented as having run away from his master three times. The dialogue represented the conversation which took place between them, when the slave was retaken the third time. In

this dialogue, the whole argument in behalf of slavery was brought forward by the master, all of which was disposed of by the slave. The slave was made to say some very smart as well as impressive things in reply to his master—things which had the desired though unexpected effect; for the conversation resulted in the voluntary emancipation of the slave on the part of the master.

The "Dialogue between Master and Slave" was originally published in 1793 in a book called *Evenings at Home, or, The Juvenile Budget Opened*, by John Aikin and his sister Anna Barbauld (whom many scholars suspect to be the author of this dialogue, given her known commitment to abolitionism). The idea was for the dialogue to be read by a family as a means of pleasure and moral instruction; Bingham saw that it could easily be adapted to a schoolroom setting. It is not hard to imagine the young Douglass saying to himself— or perhaps, when he could be sure of not being overheard, declaiming aloud—the bold words of the slave:

I was treacherously kidnapped in my own country, when following an honest occupation. I was put in chains, sold to one of your countrymen, carried by force on board his ship, brought hither, and exposed to sale like a beast in the market, where you bought me. What step in all this progress of violence and injustice can give a *right*? Was it in the villain who stole me, in the slave-merchant who tempted him to do so, or in you who encouraged the slave-merchant to bring his cargo of human cattle to cultivate your lands?

But this dialogue was not the only text in *The Columbian Orator* that moved the slave boy. "In the same book, I met with one of Sheridan's mighty speeches on and in behalf of Catholic emancipation"—that is, a speech made in the British Parliament by Richard Brinsley Sheridan, a native of Dublin, arguing that the Roman Catholic faith should no longer be suppressed in Ireland. What is fascinating is how the young Douglass, while living in the most oppressive possible circumstances, understood the dialogue and the speech, the first dealing directly with his condition and the second occupied by a very different problem in a very different place, as speaking to him with equal power and almost in a single voice:

> These were choice documents to me. I read them over and over again with unabated interest. They gave tongue to interesting thoughts of my own soul, which had frequently flashed through my mind, and died away for want of utterance. The moral which I gained from the dialogue was the power of truth over the conscience of even a slaveholder. What I got from Sheridan was a bold denunciation of slavery, and a powerful vindication of human rights.

The young Douglass greatly treasured the "Dialogue" that directly expressed his own condition, in which someone who looked like him and experienced the bondage that he experienced spoke eloquent words in his own defense; but he *also* greatly treasured the words of an Irishman speaking in the British Parliament on an issue altogether other than chattel slavery. Both documents "gave tongue to interesting thoughts of [his] own soul," which earlier had "died away for want of utterance." In precisely the same way, Peter Abrahams found, a century later, that the words of Du Bois told him something vital that he both grasped and did not grasp: "I had known this all along. But until now I had had no words to voice that knowledge." But his experience in reading the English poets had a similar revelatory power for him.

The experiences of these two men testify to the enormous power of *reading*. But the experiences of Abrahams and Douglass also show us that that power arises in some cases from likeness—from the sense that *that could be me speaking*—and from difference—*that is someone very different from me speaking*. For mental and moral health we need both. Our presentist moment overemphasizes the former and neglects the latter—or rather, rarely even acknowledges the latter. We tend to get at the need for otherness in different ways.

I wrote earlier of the Long Now Foundation, and one of its founders, the musician Brian Eno, has written about the value of thinking in terms of the "Big Here and the Long Now"—the Big Here being, you might say, *spatial* bandwidth. If that's what we want, it ought to manifest itself in an interest in other cultures—say, learning other languages, or at least reading works from other cultures in translation. Sad to say, people in the English-speaking countries, especially in the U.S.A., tend not to be very interested in other languages or the literatures written in them. But we *are* interested in First Contact—the initial human encounter with extraterrestrial intelligence. We make many, many science fiction books and movies on that theme. Which suggests that, on some level, we are fascinated by a *really* Big Here, a Here big enough to encompass the galaxy. And that's encouraging, isn't it?

Perhaps not. I'm not encouraged by that kind of Big Here any more than I am encouraged by Donna Haraway's project of "making generative oddkin" with pigeons, if it serves as a substitute for the more immediate and, well, *real* kinds of encounters. It seems that human beings have a proclivity for encountering otherness *on their own terms*— in controlled and nonthreatening ways. For instance, going to foreign countries in groups with fellow native English speakers and an English-fluent guide. And it's not as though I don't understand the impulse. I don't do tour groups, but whenever I'm in another country and try to speak the local language I get a kind of pained smile from the person I'm talking to, who shifts immediately into English. *Let's just make this easier for both of us, shall we?* I find the move to English impossible to resist: it's so easy to acquiesce, and, after all, I can tell myself that I am being polite by follow-ing my host's lead.

Perhaps even more comfortable is our cinematic expe-rience: Even if terrible things happen in some of our SF First Contact movies, they happen *in the movies*, and then we get to go home, where nothing has changed. Moreover, as Simone Weil points out in a passage I quoted early in this book, the future we imagine is just that: not an alien anything, but what *we imagine*, what we *can* imagine. And often it's what we *can't* imagine that we're most in need of.

All of these experiences point toward the value of

pursuing, seriously, a genuine engagement with the past. It is other than us in a broad range of ways, and we can't control that otherness. It speaks to us in ways that we can't understand, and then (suddenly, unexpectedly) in ways we understand perfectly. When a slave boy in Virginia reads and thrills to a speech an Irishman made in London, or when a child from the slums of Johannesburg finds his heart touched and warmed by rhymes about rural England, *that* is the Big Here and the Long Now. And that's available to all of us who have the requisite openness and patience, who are willing to risk being a bit bored, a bit confused, maybe even a bit angry. Access is easy; no systematic plan is required; the risks are low. But the rewards are potentially immense.*

The novelist and essayist Leslie Jamison has a tattoo on her arm. It's a sentence in Latin: *Homo sum, humani nihil a me alienum puto*—I am human, and nothing human is alien to me. The line is from a play by the Roman poet Terence, and Jamison's thoughts about it are interesting. First of all, when she describes it she leaves out a word: she says "I am human; nothing is alien to me," leaving out the second use of "human." I'm not sure about this: maybe what it's like to be a bat, or a pigeon, or a hawk, or a beetle, really *is* alien to me. But more important, she speaks of the changes the phrase has undergone in her mind. When she got the tattoo, she "saw it then as an articulation of empathic possibility." But that has changed a bit: "I see it now more as a sentiment that has a lot of internal tensions. How do we

---

*Whole worlds are available for the taking at Project Gutenberg: https://gutenberg.org

try to understand each other's experiences? What are the limits of that understanding? I think it's fine for sentiments to have tensions embedded inside of them. I think it's useful. It keeps them crackly, in a good way."

That's a wonderful metaphor: the *crackling* that's generated, the sparks that fly, when multiple responses to others, including others from the past, rub against each other. Terence's line is one I quote often. When I do, I always point out that Terence does not say that everything human is transparent to him, instantly accessible to him. He says it is not alien, not wholly outside the scope of his experience, not opaque to his inquiries. It puts up resistance. But that resistance, and the work we do to overcome it, are alike necessary to the task of breaking bread with the dead.

7.

THE STOICS' MOMENT

The ancient Stoics are having a moment—chiefly among men. And it's a rather weird moment.

Though it seems that not many people realize it, the first seeds of the Stoic renaissance—if we can call it that—were planted by Tom Wolfe in his sprawling 1998 novel *A Man in Full*. What's especially interesting about this novel is the way it emphasizes the connection between Stoicism and manliness. One of the chief characters in *A Man in Full* is Charlie Croker, an Atlanta real estate developer who gets himself into deep financial trouble, which leads to other kinds of trouble. The neatly stacked dominoes of Charlie's life start falling, and his ramifying failures eventually cause him to question the meaning and value of his whole life— cause him mournfully to ask whether in any meaningful sense he is still a *man*.

At this point someone comes into his life: a practical nurse helping Charlie with some of his humiliating physical ailments, a young man named Conrad Hensley. Conrad is an ex-con who went to prison because his sense of personal honor simply did not allow him to accept a plea deal—he would have had to lie, to plead guilty to something he didn't do. In prison he began to doubt the wisdom of being so upright, until by accident he came across a book containing the writings of the Greek Stoic Epictetus, a contemporary of our old friend Plutarch. The counsel that Epictetus gave convinced Conrad that he had indeed acted rightly in refusing the plea deal, because the honorable man does what is right regardless of the consequences to himself.

> Only Epictetus understood. He *understood*! Only he understood why Conrad Hensley had refused to accept a plea bargain! Only Epictetus understood why he had refused to lower himself just a rung or two, demean himself just a little bit, dishonor himself just a touch, confess to a minor crime, a mere misdemeanor, in order to avoid the risk of a jail sentence.

This is amazing to Conrad. "Epictetus *spoke* to him!—from half a world and two thousand years away!" (The Big Here and the Long Now.)

Moreover, Conrad came to see that in the writings of Epictetus lay something else, something greater: a whole philosophy of life; a reliable guide to decision making in good times and bad. And Conrad shares this philosophy with Charlie.

Obviously the philosophy of Epictetus and the other Stoics is detailed, but for Conrad and Charlie this is the heart of it:

What Epictetus had to say was supremely simple, and he said it over and over again in different ways. All human beings are the children of Zeus, who has given them a spark of his divine fire. Once you have that spark, no one, not even Zeus, can take it from you. This spark gives you the faculty of reasoning and the will to act or not to act and the will to get and the will to avoid. But the will to get and avoid what? "To get what is good," says Epictetus, "and to avoid what is evil." There is no use spending your life agonizing over the things that are not dependent upon your will, such as money, possessions, fame, and political power. Likewise, there is no use spending your life trying to avoid the things that are not dependent upon your will, such as the tyranny of a Nero, imprisonment, and physical danger. (Conrad nodded as he read it.) Epictetus had a special scorn for those who "merely tremble and mourn and seek to escape misfortune."

It is this message that Conrad shares with poor, humiliated, formerly rich, formerly strong, formerly masterful Charlie Croker. Will Charlie lie and connive to "escape misfortune"? Or will he recognize the spark of divinity within himself and act in accordance with its intrinsic dignity?

A Man in Full put Stoicism on the cultural map for a brief time around the turn of the millennium, but attention to it faded, as our attention is wont to do. But in recent years the Stoics have returned and have been appropriated by people whose use of them is rather different from Conrad Hensley's. Which brings us to what some have called the *manosphere*—the corner of the internet made by men for men and in support of a very particular understanding of what it means to be a man.

Donna Zuckerberg, a classicist and the founder of the online classics journal *Eidolon*, spent a good deal of time—more time than I can think of without a shudder—exploring how a kind of online men's culture built itself on a framework of classical ideas, especially those of the Stoics. Her reporting is fascinating, but, as I hope to show, her response to the classicist manosphere is not altogether convincing.

Zuckerberg is especially interested in a diffuse group she refers to as the Red Pill Stoics. Many in the manosphere believe that they, like Neo in *The Matrix*, have disdained the Blue Pill that keeps them intellectually sedated and have opted instead for the Red Pill that shows them what the world is really like. People who have taken the Blue Pill believe in feminism and multiculturalism and racial equality—all the ideas they are consistently being sold through the media. Those who have taken the Red Pill believe they see those ideas as the illusions they truly are; and the question for them now becomes how to flourish, especially as straight white men, in an environment designed to malign and marginalize them.

The online Red Pill communities therefore focus a good deal of their attention on self-help. Says Zuckerberg, "Many men are attracted to the Red Pill not only because it provides them with a community of other like-minded men, but also because they are seeking advice on how to improve themselves." And that's where the Stoics come in. "Stoicism focuses explicitly on self-improvement, so it can be blended easily into the self-help aspect of Red Pill communities." She notes that in his *On Anger* the Roman philosopher Seneca asks his readers to do a daily self-evaluation to determine whether they are making progress in combating their vices. (Just to show that the current interest in the Stoics goes far beyond the manosphere, I note that a new edition of Seneca's treatise has recently been published by Princeton University Press under the title *How to Keep Your Cool: An Ancient Guide to Anger Management*. Indeed, Princeton has a whole series called "Ancient Wisdom for Modern Readers." More on this later.)

Again and again Zuckerberg juxtaposes the Red Pill interpretations of the Stoics to what the Stoics actually wrote, with sometimes jarring and sometimes ludicrous results. For instance, some discomfort is caused in the Red Pill community by the fact that Epictetus was in his early life a slave. Worse still, he was known to be lame, and indeed many later commentators claimed that his leg had been deliberately broken by his master, a secretary to the Emperor Nero. To a community that believes in physical fitness and demonstrations of overt muscular prowess, none of this looks good *at all*. Is there a way to salvage Epictetus's reputation?

One skeptical non-Stoic commentator wasn't so sure. "Maybe Epictetus could have prevented his master from breaking his leg if he [had] tried to stir up some doubts in the master's mind by targeted questions." Ah yes, *targeted questions*—those powerful instruments of deliverance from servitude. But the Red Pill Stoics not only defended Epictetus, they saw his situation as providing some much-needed wisdom for our current moment. If black people, for instance, believe that, thanks to their centuries of enslavement on this continent and the subsequent history of racial prejudice both overt (Jim Crow laws, redlining) and implicit (job recruiters downgrading "black" names), they continue to be economically disadvantaged, they certainly should not be seeking legal remedies such as reparations. Rather, they should follow the example of Epictetus and make good philosophical use of their suffering. Epictetus didn't let enslavement and physical abuse get in his way—why should black Americans? The problem here is not enslavement, it's how you *react* to being a slave.

So Zuckerberg convincingly demonstrates that the Stoicism of the Red Pillers is little more than a kind of costuming or window dressing: they mine the Stoics only in order to find ancient confirmation of what they already believe to be true and want to see done, and they ignore what doesn't fit. Zuckerberg does the same kind of work in relation to other ancient traditions that have an afterlife in certain corners of the internet: for instance, the would-be ladies' men who read Ovid's *Ars Amatoria* (*The Art of Love*) as a straightforward seduction manual. The manosphere is repeatedly shown to be insensitive, indeed profoundly resistant, to historical difference.

And yet, while I *greatly* prefer Zuckerberg's readings of these old writers to those that emerge from the manosphere, I wonder if she doesn't have a similar problem.

Early in her book she writes, "By analyzing and deconstructing this Red Pill enthusiasm for ancient Greece and Rome, I hope to articulate a different vision for a feminist, radical place that classical antiquity can occupy in contemporary political discourse." And then in the chapter on Stoicism: "Through understanding how and why Stoicism appeals to the reactionary tendencies of the men who frequent Red Pill websites, we can also determine what in the philosophy can help promote progressive gender politics and social activism." This sounds like being interested in ancient literature and philosophy only insofar as that interest serves the politics of the moment—and in that sense, Zuckerberg actually agrees with the Red Pill Stoics about what reading old books is *for*. She merely has different political ends than they do.

In this model, whether employed by the right or the left or by some other political agenda that doesn't fit on that scale, the books of the past may well be useful *instruments* but they cannot be our *teachers*. They cannot teach us in part because we are refusing to listen to what they have to say that doesn't fit into our preexisting categories.

A different example may help me to illustrate this point. Massimo Pigliucci, a professor of philosophy at City University of New York, has recently published a book called *How to Be a Stoic: Using Ancient Philosophy to Live a Modern Life*. He says that he himself was increasingly drawn to Stoicism because he finds in it "a rational, science-friendly philosophy that includes a metaphysics with a spiritual dimension, is explicitly open to revision, and, most importantly, is eminently practical." But Pigliucci is not just *interested*: he says flatly, "I've become a Stoic," which he understands in this way: "in practice Stoicism involves a dynamic combination of reflecting on theoretical precepts, reading inspirational texts, and engaging in meditation, mindfulness, and other spiritual exercises."

The only problem with this, says Carlos Fraenkel in an incisive review of *How to Be a Stoic*, is that what Pigliucci describes simply isn't Stoicism. Says Fraenkel, "Pigliucci contends . . . that living well in the Stoic sense doesn't depend 'on whether there is a God' or what God's 'specific attributes' are. I strongly disagree." Fraenkel thinks that the Stoic model of living well depends *wholly* on what it believes about God. "For the Stoics, Zeus made everything, including human beings, to maximize the universe's perfection. What sets human beings apart is that they alone share in Zeus's rational nature and can help carry out his plan by embracing the fate he has allotted to them." No one would practice the hard disciplines of Stoicism—the kinds of disciplines that made it possible for young Epictetus to accept his enslavement, and even horrific physical abuse, as long as it lasted—unless they believed that a good God had perfectly ordered the world. Pigliucci says that the Stoics tried to make the world better; *No they didn't,* replies Fraenkel, because they thought it was already perfect. "The key to happiness, therefore, is human reason, which enables us to understand Zeus's plan and then direct our lives in accordance with it." I don't think Fraenkel would be so critical if Pigliucci had said that he had learned a lot from Stoicism; but "I've become a Stoic" is for Fraenkel a bridge too far.

My first inclination, when I read Fraenkel's review, was to think that he was being too persnickety. But the more I thought about it the more satisfied I became with his insistence, because it really is far too easy for us to map old books and their authors onto our familiar, comfortable categories—"inspirational texts," "meditation, mindfulness, and other spiritual exercises"—a mapping that renders us unable to hear a strange word, a different word, a word that takes us beyond what we already know.

Earlier in this book I commented that I do not think we should suspend our moral commitments when we read old texts—we need not keep an open mind about whether Petruchio might be right to "tame" Kate the "shrew"—but I do think we should make an effort to bracket our *categories*. Just this is what Mark Lilla has argued that we need to do in order to be fair to the writers of the past: "when approaching the past we often apply concepts and categories—religion, race, the individual—that were not available to those living then, and so we fail to understand them as they understood themselves." C. V. Wedgwood—who, as my favorite historian, has turned up several times in these pages—has quite explicitly stated that this was the aim of her historical writing: She says of the first volume of her history of the English Civil War, "This book is not a defence of one side or the other, not an economic analysis, not a social study; it is an attempt to understand how these men felt and why, *in their own estimation*, they acted as they did" (emphasis mine). Wedgwood freely acknowledges that this isn't the only valid way to write history: "It is legitimate for the historian to pierce the surface and bring to light motives and influences not known at the time; but it is equally legitimate to accept the motives and explanations which satisfied contemporaries." In fact, she says, both approaches are necessary; neither should be "accepted as the whole truth." Wedgwood clearly, and rightly, felt that the historians of her time were so devoted to offering explanations from above, as it were, in language that the people of the time studied not only wouldn't have accepted but wouldn't have understood, that they had lost any sense of the value of depicting what she calls the "immediacy of experience." She thinks it's a valuable exercise to project ourselves imaginatively into the mental and emotional world of people from the past: not to think of what *we* would do if we were in that situation, but of how that experience felt, immediately, to *them*, to people shaped and formed as they were. Here we might recall, from the first pages of this book, Amitav Ghosh's use of pre-modern Bengali literature to illuminate the "immediacy of experience" of those exposed to the ravages of an ever-changing natural world.

As Lilla suggests, embracing that immediacy, striving to understand the people of the past "as they understood themselves," is a mark of fairness to them; but it is also good for us. He points out that "the concept of 'racism' is today applied to everything from theories of racial inferiority and calls for genocide to unintended 'microaggressions' against particular individuals," which means that "a small forest of useful concepts that used to grow between 'racism' and 'woke-ness'—blindness, stereotyping, prejudice, bigotry—has been cleared. Consequently, we are losing the ability to understand how people in the past thought about their attitudes and actions, and therefore are losing the ability to make proportionate moral judgments." That we simplify our judgments in the cause of triage, the management of information overload, is understandable, but the resulting impulsiveness leaves us unable to count, or even to acknowledge, the costs of our simplifications. We thereby become uncharitable to our ancestors—*and* to ourselves, whom we are depriving of one of the most vital traits imaginable: "the ability to make proportionate moral judgments."

In a brilliant essay on the same branches of the online alt-right that Donna Zuckerberg covers, Brian Phillips quotes a compelling line by Emily Dickinson: "The unknown is the largest need of the intellect." Phillips continues, "I happen to believe that this is true; but the kind of esotericism that thrives on the far right has never had the slightest interest in the unknown. It wants to be told the news it wants to hear." But this is not a pitfall to which the right alone is subject. Any one of us who denies that we want our assumptions confirmed would be lying or self-deceived. The theater critic Terry Teachout talks about plays that flatter their audience, that reassure them that the beliefs they came into the playhouse with are the ones with which they should leave: he calls this the "theater of concurrence." The concluding lines of Phillips's essay make, I think, a fitting commentary on this chapter, because *all* of us, on some level, want the whole world to be for us a theater of concurrence: "The varieties of false knowledge in this world are infinite; one of the most dangerous is the knowledge that answers desire. Policies begin in dreams."

Indeed they do. And to understand how this works, we should return to a figure from earlier in our story, Frederick Douglass. His reflection on the American Founders—in a speech called "The Meaning of July Fourth for the Negro" delivered in Rochester, New York, on July 4, 1852—is as excellent an example of reckoning healthily with the past as anything I have ever read. He begins by acknowledging that "they were great men," though he immediately goes on to say, "The point from which I am compelled to view them is not, certainly, the most favorable; and yet I cannot contemplate their great deeds with less than admiration." Yes: Douglass is *compelled* to view them in a critical light, because their failure to eradicate slavery at the nation's founding led to his own enslavement, led to his being beaten and abused and denied every human right, forced him to live in bondage and in fear until he could at long last make his escape. Nevertheless, "for the good they did, and the principles they contended for, I will unite with you to honor their memory."

What could possibly have been so noble about the Founders to Douglass? First, "They loved their country better than their own private interests," which is good; though they were "peace men," "they preferred revolution to peaceful submission to bondage," which is very good, and indeed true of Douglass himself; and "With them, nothing was 'settled' that was not right," which is excellent. Perhaps best of all, "With them, justice, liberty and

humanity were 'final;' not slavery and oppression." Therefore, "You may well cherish the memory of such men. They
were great in their day and generation."

In their day and generation. But what they achieved,
though astonishing in its time, can no longer be deemed
adequate. Indeed it never could have been so deemed,
because they had not lived up to the principles they so
powerfully celebrated. They had announced a "final"—
that is, an absolute, a nonnegotiable—commitment to justice, liberty, and humanity, and even those who did not
own slaves themselves negotiated away the rights of black
people. And so—here Douglass moves from the introduction of his speech to the meat of it—he must say these
blunt words: "This Fourth July is yours, not mine. You may
rejoice, I must mourn."

For every time he hears the Founders praised, he hears
something else too:

> Fellow-citizens, above your national, tumultuous joy, I
> hear the mournful wail of millions, whose chains, heavy
> and grievous yesterday, are, today, rendered more intol-
> erable by the jubilee shouts that reach them. . . . To
> forget them, to pass lightly over their wrongs, and to
> chime in with the popular theme, would be treason
> most scandalous and shocking, and would make me a
> reproach before God and the world. My subject, then,
> fellow-citizens, is American slavery.

If I had been there at that moment the hair would have stood
on the back of my neck; indeed it sometimes does so even
when I just read the words.

I wonder whether I can even imagine what it *cost* Douglass to speak so warmly of the Founders. This is something we can only begin to understand by reflecting on two key passages in his autobiography. In the first, he tells the story of how the wife of his master taught him to read—until the master himself put a stop to it, and prophesied that Douglass would someday regret his own literacy. Then, sometime later, when he encounters *The Columbian Orator* and its moving depictions of enslavement and injustice, he felt his emotions continually rising: "The more I read, the more I was led to abhor and detest my enslavers. I could regard them in no other light than a band of successful robbers, who had left their homes, and gone to Africa, and stolen us from our homes, and in a strange land reduced us to slavery. I loathed them as being the meanest as well as the most wicked of men." And thus "that very discontentment which Master Hugh had predicted would follow my learning to read had already come, to torment and sting my soul to unutterable anguish. As I writhed under it, I would at times feel that learning to read had been a curse rather than a blessing."

The Founders could not have been exempt from this loathing: after all, some of them owned slaves, and were among those "who had left their homes, and gone to Africa, and stolen us from our homes, and in a strange land reduced us to slavery." They deserved denunciation no less than the men who had claimed ownership of Douglass. And yet, in his Rochester speech, he had conquered his indignation sufficiently to say: "They were great in their day and generation."

How could this acknowledgment not have been costly to Douglass? He had every reason to hate the Founders for their corruption or cowardice. And yet while justly reprobating them for the failures that led to his enslavement and that of millions of his sisters and brothers, he also acknowledges the role that the principles they articulated played in allowing the abolitionist movement to emerge. Even in this he is measured: in his final paragraph, in which he declares "I do not despair of this country," he gives those principles some of the credit—but not all, and maybe not even much of it. "While drawing encouragement from 'the Declaration of Independence,' the great principles it contains, and the genius of American Institutions, my spirit is also cheered by the obvious tendencies of the age." He discerns a vast social and spiritual wind of freedom blowing through the country, and if the Declaration of Independence blows in the same direction, it is not the *cause* of the current weather.

It would be utterly unjust to demand of anyone wounded as Douglass was wounded the charity he exhibits here. I would not ever dare to *ask* it. That he speaks as warmly of the Founders as he does strikes me as little less than a miracle. But this almost ostentatious fairmindedness was integral to Douglass's massive success as an orator, as a persuader of the half-convinced and the faint of heart. It is a model of reckoning with the past, to sift, to assess, to return and reflect again. The idealization and demonization of the past are equally easy, and immensely tempting in an age of social acceleration. What Douglass offers instead is a model of *negotiating* with the past in a way that gives charity and honesty equal weight.

I do not tell you that this is an easy task; I do not even tell you that it is one with which you can be finished. If you think as Douglass thought, you will never reach a final ver- dict on those who came before you; you will at best agree to a continuation. And it is in agreeing to a continuation with the past, not in pronouncing a universal verdict either for or against, a simple thumbs-up or thumbs-down, that we increase our personal density.

8

The View from
the Doll's House

—————

I vividly remember the first time I heard a parent say that
she thought she and her husband should choose a mate
for their daughter. (The moment is memorable largely because that first time has, so far, been the only time.) My
initial thought was *You're completely insane.* That was also
my second and third thought, but reflecting on the encounter later I finally had a different thought, which was
How do I know you're completely insane? And that question led
me down a curious path of thought.

The woman's core argument was this: Young people are
both hormone-afflicted and inexperienced, and that's a
combination of traits poorly suited to spouse selection.
Better to allow their more knowledgeable and less emo-
tionally invested parents to sift through the options and
come up with the best fit for long-term satisfaction. Which
(I thought) might be at least a defensible idea if those parents are as levelheaded as all that. But what if they happen

to have priorities other than the happiness of their children? Or their idea of happiness is irreconcilably different from the children's self-understanding? Or if they choose someone whom their child finds thoroughly unattractive?

As it turned out, the woman had anticipated all of these objections. She freely acknowledged that marriages made by parents could go wrong, and in exactly the ways that had leaped to my mind. But the question, she said, was not whether her model is perfect; it was whether her model was better than the one our society currently employs. Look at the state of marriage in this country, she said. Look at how many marriages fail. Look at how many young people, who see how many marriages fail, choose not to marry at all. It's time to try something different. She even thought that, if we could clear away some of the widely distributed propaganda about Romantic Love, young people might come to embrace the idea, to appreciate being relieved of the burden of making a choice they don't know how to make well.

I'm sure all of us have at some time had the experience I had then: being overwhelmed by having to confront an idea we had never considered—being at a loss, argumentatively, not because the person arguing with us is necessarily correct, but because that person has reflected on something we've never reflected on. Until that woman suggested her plan to me, I had never considered that there could be a serious alternative to our current model: two individuals choosing to marry each other on the basis of . . . well, whatever they thought was most important, I guess. On even two minutes' reflection the whole system suddenly seemed ramshackle, maybe even untenable. Why had its shortcomings never occurred to me before?

I thought about Romeo and Juliet, who fit our norm, but then I also thought about Odysseus and Penelope—how did *they* find each other? I realized that I had no idea what Homer's audiences would have expected, what their assumptions (probably as unconscious and unconsidered as my own) would have been. And I thought about a real woman, an Englishwoman who lived about three and a half centuries ago. Her name was Dorothy Osborne.

Once upon a time, in seventeenth-century England, there was a man named William Temple, who became a noted British diplomat. He was sufficiently distinguished that a writer named Thomas Peregrine Courtenay composed one of those hefty Victorian biographies of him in 1838. Courtenay's *Life of Sir William Temple* had the misfortune to fall into the hands of the brilliant historian, journalist, and polemicist Lord Macaulay, who tore it to shreds in the pages of the *Edinburgh Review*—but one aspect of the book appealed to Macaulay: the Appendix, in which Courtenay had placed some of the letters written to Temple by a woman who loved him: Dorothy Osborne. "Mr. Courtenay expresses some doubt whether his readers will think him justified in inserting so large a number of these epistles," Macaulay declared. "We only wish there were twice as many." Macaulay's enthusiasm in turn intrigued a certain Edward Abbott Parry, who tracked down the whole cache of letters and published an edition of them.

The story of William Temple and Dorothy Osborne is worthy of enshrinement in a cinematic historical romance.

They met and fell passionately in love in 1645, in the midst of England's Civil War, with fathers on opposite sides: Sir John Temple supported Oliver Cromwell and served in the Long Parliament, while Sir Peter Osborne, lieutenant governor of the island of Guernsey, so passionately loved King Charles that he was the last Royalist leader to surrender, yielding Castle Cornet to Parliamentary forces only when his men were starving. Even after the war's conclusion, neither family was pleased by the prospect of Dorothy and William's union.

Dorothy was beset by a flock of suitors, the most noteworthy of whom was Henry Cromwell, son of that dreadful rebel who would soon become Lord Protector of England. The Osbornes, who were short of cash at the time, felt they could scarcely afford to stand on ideological principle. Dorothy's brother Henry—who seems to have been the de facto head of the family—was especially eager for the match. But, even when he allowed himself some political flexibility in relation to Henry Cromwell, he could not bear to think of William Temple as a suitor for his sister. It was, he thought, more a matter of character than politics. As Dorothy reported to her beloved, her brother said "that religion or honor were things that you did not consider at all, and that he was confident you would take any engagement, serve in any employment, or do anything to advance yourself." This intense familial opposition prolonged the courtship for about eight years, though neither Dorothy nor William seems to have wavered in their commitment.

The letters of Dorothy's that survive (none of William's

do) cover the courtship's last two years. I will say flatly that they are among the very greatest letters written in the English language; and I will say equally flatly that Osborne is a match for Jane Austen—yes, *Jane Austen*—in wit. I cannot sustain those extreme claims without quoting rather extensively from her letters, which I shall now proceed to do.

Here's a characteristic passage from a letter written in the summer of 1653, in which, as is habitual with her, she refers to her suitors as her "servants":

> My brother says not a word of you, nor your service, nor do I expect he should; if I could forget you, he would not help my memory. You would laugh, sure, if I could tell you how many servants he has offered me since he came down; but one above all the rest I think he is in love with himself, and may marry him too if he pleases, I shall not hinder him. 'Tis one Talbot, the finest gentleman he has seen this seven year; but the mischief on't is he has not above fifteen or sixteen hundred pound a year, though he swears he begins to think one might bate £500 a year for such a husband. I tell him I am glad to hear it; and if I were as much taken [as he] with Mr. Talbot, I should not be less gallant; but I doubted the first extremely.

In addition to poor Talbot we find, in the same letter, an appearance by one of the recurrent characters in the epistolary saga: Sir Justinian Isham, a widower with five children (four of them daughters) who seems to have had a reputation for piety but whom Dorothy thinks "the vainest, impertinent, self-conceited learned coxcomb that ever yet I saw." She invariably refers to him as "the Emperor Justinian" and describes her encounters with him in diplomatic terms: "Would you think it, that I have an ambassador from the Emperor Justinian that comes to renew the treaty? In earnest, 'tis true, and I want your counsel extremely, what to do in it. You told me once that of all my servants you liked him the best. If I could do so too, there were no dispute in't. Well, I'll think on't, and if it succeed I will be as good as my word; you shall take your choice of my four daughters."

Osborne excels at such banter, but in the most remarkable of her letters, the power comes from an extraordinary moment of Christian reconciliation. It begins when Henry's vitriolic condemnation of Temple's character finally became too much for Dorothy, who up to this point has cheerfully ignored her brother's attacks:

> I had not patience for this. To say you were a beggar, your father not worth 4000 in the whole world, was nothing in comparison of having no religion nor no honor. I forgot all my disguise, and we talked ourselves weary; he renounced me again, and I defied him, but both in as civil language as it would permit, and parted in great anger with the usual ceremony of a leg and a courtesy, that you would have died with laughing to have seen us.

But this was not the end of the story.

> The next day I, not being at dinner, saw him not till night; then he came into my chamber. . . . [He] sat

half-an-hour and said not one word, nor I to him. At last, in a pitiful tone, "Sister," says he, "I have heard you say that when anything troubles you, of all things you apprehend going to bed, because there it increases upon you, and you lie at the mercy of all your sad thoughts, which the silence and darkness of the night adds a horror to; I am at that pass now. I vow to God I would not endure another night like the last to gain a crown."

And from that admission by the proud and haughty Henry, peace between brother and sister was restored.

[We] fell into a discourse of melancholy and the causes, and from that (I know not how) into religion; and we talked so long of it, and so devoutly, that it [allayed] all our anger. We grew to a calm and peace with all the world. Two hermits conversing in a cell they equally inhabit, never expressed more humble, charitable kindness, one towards another, than we. He asked my pardon and I his, and he has promised me never to speak of it to me whilst he lives, but leave the event to God Almighty; and till he sees it done, he will be always the same to me that he is; then he shall leave me, he says, not out of want of kindness to me, but because he cannot see the ruin of a person that he loves so passionately, and in whose happiness he had laid up all his. These are the terms we are at, and I am confident he will keep his word with me, so that you have no reason to fear him in any respect.

The tribulations of the courtship were not over even with this. After all the "servants" had been sent away and the families (however imperfectly) reconciled to the match, Dorothy contracted smallpox, which left her face disfigured by scars, her beauty gone. William's love survived this last trial, and they were married at Christmas 1654. Dorothy's death parted them forty-one years later. William outlived her by four years.

As vividly and movingly as Osborne can describe the dark nights of her soul, she always retains a healthy distance from even her deepest fears: the great constant in her prose is the wit that enables her to see the humor and absurdity of our affairs. Indeed, for those many difficult and uncertain years when she and Temple were separated, wit must have been her chief tool for emotional survival. She was one of the great chroniclers of the human comedy. But few other than me would rate her nearly so highly. Why is that?

Partly because she wrote only letters, and we do not think of letters as having the same literary status as novels or epic poems. Yet there are several writers, especially in the century following Osborne, who dedicated themselves to letter writing as a vital literary genre, who expected to be remembered as masters of that art. That is a bridge for us to cross if we want to appreciate Osborne; but it's crossable.

A larger and more treacherous bridge is this: Osborne's lack of interest in what we might think of as feminist concerns. Many of the writers published in, for example, the distinguished and scholarly Oxford Women Writers series exemplify a kind of proto-feminism, but Osborne seems to have had little in common with these authors. Indeed, in one letter she scoffs at the literary ambitions of Margaret Cavendish, the Duchess of Newcastle: "Sure, the poor woman is a little distracted, she could never be so ridiculous else as to venture at writing books, and in verse too. If I should not sleep this fortnight I should not come to that." And indeed, once Osborne and Temple were safely married, the flow of letters seems to have stopped—because why write if the one who had inspired your writing now shares your bed and your breakfast table?

So Dorothy Osborne is a complicated case for the modern reader. She insisted on the freedom to choose her husband in defiance of her family's ideas of what was best for her, and she articulated her insistence in brilliant English prose. To that degree she embraces what we think of as a proper model of Romantic Love—which is why I commented that her story would make a wonderful movie. Yet she placed no particular value on her gifts as a writer, thought the very idea of a woman writing books an absurdity, and simply wanted to be married and to bear her beloved's children.

The situation might create some cognitive dissonance for us. Do we practice negative selection and stop listening to her because of her acceptance of a culture in which the scriptures say "wives, obey your husbands"? Or do we set that aside and practice positive selection, and welcome Osborne into the household of writers we admire because of the spirit and wit with which she resisted her brother's claimed dominance over her and insisted on following her own path to love?

It's interesting, I think, to ask whether we would feel

any differently about Osborne if she had taken something like the opposite path. What if she had meekly and obediently married the Emperor Justinian—but then refused to obey him and devoted her time to writing books, like the Duchess of Newcastle? Readers differ, but I think that alternate-universe Dorothy Osborne would seem a more modern figure to us, and perhaps a more sympathetic one. A bit like Nora Helmer.

Henrik Ibsen's play *A Doll's House* was one of the sensations of the nineteenth century because of its portrayal of Nora Helmer, a wife and mother who ultimately finds the confines of bourgeois life unbearable and leaves her family. Even the suggestion that Nora might be right to do so was outrageous at the time—so much so that one of Ibsen's contemporaries said that the play "pronounced a death sentence on accepted social ethics."

Indeed, when the play was first performed in Germany the famous actress playing Nora refused to perform the final scene: "*I* would never leave *my* children!" Since Ibsen had no copyright laws to protect his play, and anyone could change it in any way they wished, he, with gritted teeth, wrote an alternate ending in which Nora, on the verge of departing her home, is forced to look into her children's bedroom, whereupon she sinks to the floor in mute acknowledgment that *she* could never leave *her* children. Fade to black. Ibsen called this ending a "barbaric outrage" upon his play, but figured that changes made by other hands would have been even worse.

In 2017, a new play reached Broadway: *A Doll's House, Part 2*, by Lucas Hnath, which revisits Nora and her family fifteen years after she walked out of the "doll's house" in which she had been kept by her husband, slamming the door behind her. And in Hnath's sequel Nora is very glad that she left her husband and children all those years ago.

To which Terry Teachout said: Well of course. Can you imagine a play on Broadway in 2017 suggesting that Nora perhaps should have swallowed her frustrations and remained to raise her children? This review is the origin of the "theater of concurrence" phrase I used in the previous chapter:

> The favorable reception of *A Doll's House, Part 2* was as much a foregone conclusion as is its ending, which is a quintessential example of what I call the "theater of concurrence," a genre whose practitioners take for granted that their liberal audiences already agree with them about everything. The success of such plays is contingent on the exactitude with which the author tells his audience what it wants to hear, and Hnath obliges in every particular. Above all, the viewer is never allowed to doubt that Nora was right to abandon her family for the sake of her own fulfillment.

I haven't seen the play, but I have read it, and I don't think Teachout is right about Hnath—though he may well be right about the performance he saw. Reading Hnath's play I found myself disliking Nora very much, especially the way she recasts her abandonment of her family in terms of heroic sacrifice. For instance, she tells the family's servant

Anne Marie about the great personal "discipline" she had to exercise in order to prevent herself from sending Christmas presents to the three children she left without a mother. *How brave of you, Nora!* (Later, when Anne Marie tells Nora it was terrible for her to leave her children, Nora replies that it's not a big deal, men leave their families all the time.)

And there's a powerful moment when Nora meets her daughter Emmy—the daughter who doesn't remember her because she was so young when Nora left. Emmy knows that Nora has written books denouncing the institution of marriage, and so is reluctant to tell Nora that she herself is engaged. "You think no one should get married," she says, which Nora at first denies, but then goes into a lecture about how "Marriage is this binding contract, and love is— love has to be the opposite of a contract—love needs to be free." And when Emmy resists this:

> NORA: How much do you even know about marriage?
> EMMY: Nothing.
> NORA: Exactly.
> EMMY: Because you left, I know nothing about what a marriage is and what it looks like. But I do know what the absence of it looks like, and what I want is the opposite of that.

And ultimately Emmy forces Nora to admit that the only reason Nora is speaking to her is to enlist her help in getting Torvald, her husband, to give Nora a formal divorce.

This does not, to me, look like a situation in which "the viewer is never allowed to doubt that Nora was right to abandon her family for the sake of her own fulfillment."

You could perhaps *play it* that way. You could do something to make Emmy unattractive—in fact, perhaps the only way to make Nora seem unquestionably right is to make every other character in the play seem unquestionably awful—but Hnath's writing does not hand you that interpretation on a platter. (Very much the same is true of his earlier play *The Christians*, whose pastor protagonist takes a stand that every good liberal will admire but may also be a selfish and calculating jerk.) If the director and cast of the performance Teachout saw managed to make the play's meaning unambiguous, then that's a sign of how desperately the performers as well as the viewers of plays can feel the need for a theater of concurrence—even when the playwright wants to deny them that comfort.

Near the beginning of this book I talked about the ways that information overload generates the need for informational triage. That environment also creates the need for *moral* triage: for straightforward binary decisions about whether we admire or despise a given person. Admiring is easier when a person embodies values that stand high on our list of priorities—especially if we think that those priorities are being threatened. It is likely that, among the company staging *A Doll's House, Part 2* and among its Broadway audiences, a good many people believe that a *Handmaid's Tale*–style misogynist theocracy, with fundamentalist Christian men enslaving women to fixed roles as Handmaids and Aunts and Marthas, could emerge if we are not vigilant. If so, then—in light of our earlier discussion of the situations in which we are disinclined to acknowledge that even vitally necessary progress comes with costs—we are sure to find among those people a strong inclination to support Nora's choice and to minimize the costs of it. Presumably Lucas Hnath wrote the play *because* it raises questions that are germane to our moment—but the questions germane to our moment are precisely the ones that are hardest for us to assess fairly, because of our emotional investment in them. (As D. T. Max comments in a profile of Hnath, "The hallmark of a Hnath script is robust argument, but these debates are always infused by the stormy relationships around them.") That is where the theater of concurrence comes from: it encourages us in the feeling that we've reached the proper conclusions on the issues involved and therefore don't need to revisit them—and a good feeling it is, because heaven knows there's already enough for us to think about. Once more we perceive the power of triage.

So in light of Hnath's play we can see that, from our perspective if not from his, Ibsen rather let himself off the hook by ending *A Doll's House* where he did. He didn't have to reflect on the costs and consequences of Nora's decision to leave because all he had to do was to show us that such a decision could be psychologically plausible and at the very least not *necessarily* immoral. That was the idea that had to be raised in his time: that human beings—even women!—have the right to self-determination and are not morally *required* to set aside their own well-being for the sake of the social order into which they happen to be born.

That particular lesson we have learned so well that it can be hard to remember that it *had to be* learned. Which can take the steam out of a performance today of *A Doll's*

House: yes, yes, we think, of course Nora is right to declare her independence. What was in its time a drama of profound tension can become in our own a mere melodrama, in which we already know who to root for. I have a suspicion that Lucas Hnath wrote a sequel to the story in order to revivify those characters: and it has the interesting side effect of making Ibsen's original drama stand forth more brightly, to make its original question—Does this woman dare to escape her doll's house?—seem alive again. As though we had *not* answered it definitively.

These *complications of perception* are essential to the value of reading the past—they are the chief means, I think, by which increasing our temporal bandwidth increases our personal density. Yes, there is a cost to this, and we have to fight our triage instincts to get to the point of experiencing, along with the people of the past, the choices that shaped their lives. We see their moral frames continually coming in and out of focus: at one moment we feel that we know them intimately and at the next scarcely at all. Think of how the modern reader feels about Dorothy Osborne's determination to marry the person she loves, and then about her contemptuous disdain for women who write books.

Helen Lewis, when she was coming toward the end of writing a book on the history of feminism, commented,

> I can finally see why historians are so evangelical about what they do: studying history completely reframes how you see the present. A dozen times during the research, I found that a thought I believed was original had been expressed beautifully by a woman

in the 1850s, or 1910s, or 1970s. It has made me feel
more connected to feminism as a tradition, but also
furious with myself for taking the long way round
when other women had hacked a path through the
weeds for me, if only I had known.

This is wonderfully true and powerful; but there's something also to be said for that moment when a figure from
the past who has perfectly anticipated something you already believe then turns around and says something that
puzzles or alienates you. *That* is, I firmly believe, the greater
moment of enlightenment: the moment of double realization. To confront the reality that the very same people who
give us rich wisdom can also talk what seems to us absolute
nonsense (and vice versa) is an education in the human condition. Including our own condition, which is likewise
compounded of wisdom and nonsense.

A 2019 episode of the radio program *This American Life*
tells the story of a woman named Shamyla, whose
Pakistan-born parents raised her in suburban Maryland.
They were her adoptive parents: she had actually been born
to her mother's sister, who had several children, and, in
keeping with a common custom, gave one of hers to her
childless sibling. Later, the sister who had been unable to
conceive got pregnant, twice, and gave birth to two boys.

When Shamyla was twelve, she traveled to Pakistan to
visit her extended family in Peshawar, and when she arrived they decided to keep her. She was their child, they

said; they also said that the parents who had taken her in didn't really love her, they loved only their boys, their "real" children. Also, it was clear that if she were raised in America she would become immoral, faithless, apostate. Her "real" family would therefore raise her as a faithful Muslim girl—according to their understanding of what Islam is—even though they knew that she had so many bad American habits that her reeducation would be painful for everyone concerned. And they could do this because Shamyla's adoption had never been formalized: in the eyes of Pakistani law, she was with her true family there in Peshawar and those distant Americans had no claim upon her. So the project of transforming Shamyla began.

She had to learn to cover her head, of course, and not to look men in the eye. She had to make herself marriageable, which meant, her new family believed, that she needed to get thinner, so they installed a lock on the refrigerator so she couldn't raid it. The books that she had brought with her were sure to corrupt her, and besides, a woman who reads is not attractive; so they took the books away and did not replace them. Shamyla loved to write stories, but this was perhaps worse than reading: her old/new father took her journals into the backyard and forced her to watch him burn them. She had to learn new ways, new duties; when she did not obey, she would be beaten. And so her life in Peshawar began.

But one day when she was visiting a market with a friend—she was at least allowed to have friends—she saw something that caught her attention. At one stall there was a stack of books, books in English, cheap imports from Singapore. And one of the books was Louisa May Alcott's *Little Women*, which Shamyla remembered reading, and loving, back in Maryland, in her previous life. She asked the friend to buy the book for her, promising to pay her back, and she snuck it into her bedroom and hid it in her mattress. She was worried about it making too large a lump, so she disassembled the book into eight pieces, and dispersed them along the length of the mattress.

And thus Shamyla discovered her refuge. "It was the book of my life. It was the only book I had to escape. It was the only book that I had to actually read over and over again. And I kind of memorized it." It was an escape into a wholly different world: on the other side of the globe, and 150 years in the past.

And yet not *everything* was alien. When Shamyla read about the social limitations on girls who were not yet "out" in society—"Where is the use of having a lot of dresses when she isn't out yet?" says one character—she realized that that was precisely her situation as well, and that of many girls her age in Peshawar. What she could do, how she could dress, whom she could meet and speak to, all were determined by her status as a girl not yet out. And all of a sudden this book whose chief attraction had been the utter dissimilarity to her life in Peshawar—its world of talking to boys and writing stories—became dear to her in a new way: because those nineteenth-century American girls knew at least one of the constraints she knew.

Shamyla eventually made her way back to the United States and never returned to Pakistan, but the years in which *Little Women* was her only companion, her only help, her only access to a better world than the one she was forced to live in, have marked her permanently. She calls *Little Women* her Bible. Every year on her birthday she reads the chapter that corresponds to her age, and feels that that chapter might tell her something about what will befall her in the year to come. And when she struggles to make a decision, she does something that people have for centuries done with the Bible (and for that matter with Virgil's *Aeneid*): she opens the book to a random place, drops her finger like a dowsing rod onto the page, and looks to see what counsel the sacred text has for her.

We sometimes have similar mixed reactions to our own contemporaries, especially if they come from different cultures than ours. But the past brings home to us in distinctive ways the enormous range of difference in human experience. The mathematician and philosopher Alfred North Whitehead once gave very shrewd counsel to people studying the past: "Do not chiefly direct your attention to those intellectual positions which its exponents feel it necessary explicitly to defend." That is, what people in the past were openly debating and conversing about is unlikely to be the most important thing about them. "There will be some fundamental assumptions which adherents to all the variant systems within the epoch unconsciously presuppose. Such assumptions appear so obvious that people do not know what they are assuming because no other way of putting things has ever occurred to them."

And those *unarticulated* ideas are the truly key ones in any culture or age—including our own.

When we encounter real people from the past, like Dorothy Osborne, and fictional ones, like Nora Helmer in *A Doll's House* or Jo March in *Little Women*, our instinctive responses tell a tale about our values, our commitments, our assumptions, our hopes, our fears—and about theirs. When we perceive some sudden dissonance between ourselves and those people, we should not run from that dissonance but straight toward it. This testing of our responses against those of our ancestors is an exciting endeavor—a potentially endless table conversation, though, again, one we can suspend at any time. (The sad thing is that only we can benefit from it, not the ones whose world we visit.) As Leslie Jamison says, that tension crackles and sparks. And the sparks produce both light and warmth.

9

THE POET ON THE STRAND

I n his poem "Sandstone Keepsake," the Irish poet Seamus Heaney describes an evening when he was "wading a shingle beach on Inishowen"—a peninsula that juts from the northern end of County Donegal in Ireland—where he found, and kept, a "wet red stone." The stone lifted from the water on a frosty evening seemed to smoke in his hand, and this odd apparition set him thinking and remembering. His mind, populated with poems and stories and distant history, turned, oddly enough perhaps, to Guy de Montfort: a medieval English aristocrat, a murderer, one of the sinners Dante in his *Inferno* had imagined sentenced to a river of boiling blood—as though Heaney himself were standing in such a river, instead of the cold waters at the edge of the North Atlantic.

Heaney's mind may have been drawn to the past, but the poem was written in the early 1980s, during the Troubles; and the boundary between the Republic of Ireland and Northern Ireland cuts across the base of the Inishowen

peninsula. British soldiers watched that border from tow-
ers in those days, and so Heaney's poem concludes with
an emergence from reverie and reflection:

> Anyhow, there I was with the wet red stone
> in my hand, staring across at the watch-towers
> from my free state of image and allusion,
> swooped on, then dropped by trained binoculars:
> a silhouette not worth bothering about,
> out for the evening in scarf and waders
> and not about to set times wrong or right,
> stooping along, one of the venerators.

As Heaney held the wet red stone he wasn't *in* the Republic of Ireland; he dwelt in his own "free state of image
and allusion," his own populous mental world; and the British soldier with his "trained binoculars" understood that
the man "out for the evening in scarf and waders" posed no
threat: he was "not worth bothering about." Not a militant,
nor any sort of revolutionary; not even an activist; but
rather one who venerates, one who attends worshipfully to
what he loves: stones in salt water, old poems long remembered, things that can be held close as keepsakes.

But why does he think of Guy de Montfort?

Guy was born in 1244, the son of Simon de Montfort,
Earl of Leicester. When Guy was a young man, his father led
armies in the Barons' War against King Henry III, whose
claim to the throne they challenged. In May 1264 the Earl's
armies defeated those of Henry, and some began to call him
the "uncrowned King of England." But a year later, in the
Battle of Evesham, the Earl was defeated: one son was killed;

Guy and another son, also named Simon, were wounded and captured; and the Earl himself was killed and mutilated, his head, hands, feet, and testicles all severed.

Eventually the brothers Guy and Simon escaped their imprisonment and made their way to the Continent, where they offered their military services to various princes. Eventually they settled in Tuscany, where Guy was made Count of Nola. Then, in 1271, when a papal election was under way in Viterbo in the presence of several European royals, Guy and Simon arrived—and discovered their cousin Henry of Almain.

Henry had fought on the side of the king in the Barons' War, and though he had played no role in the killing of the Earl and his son—indeed had interceded with the king on behalf of his cousins the Montforts—Guy and Simon decided that this was their opportunity to take vengeance for their father and brother. They were not deterred by the fact that when they saw Henry he was at Mass, surrounded by cardinals of the Church and the kings of France and Sicily. They dragged him from the altar and murdered him before the assembled dignitaries.

The two brothers were excommunicated for their blasphemy, and neither of them lived much longer. In the seventh circle of Dante's Hell, the realm of the violent, the poet is guided for a time by a centaur, who shows us the shade of Guy:

> He pointed out a shade apart, alone:
> "In God's bosom that one clove in two
> the heart that on the Thames still drips with blood."

Henry of Almain's heart was returned to England and buried at Hailes Abbey (not on the Thames, to be precise, though not too far from its headwaters), where it "still drips with blood" because the murder remains unavenged. And even in Hell, Guy is unaccompanied, so dreadful was his act.

All this rests in the memory of a poet in scarf and waders, on a shingle beach in Inishowen, who lifts a red stone from the waters and for a moment seems to be holding in his hand the unavenged heart of Henry of Almain.

Disputed sovereignty; cousins against cousins; an apparently endless cycle of vengeance—am I speaking of the Barons' War? Or of the Irish Troubles? People in Ireland always wanted Heaney to take sides, to join the revolution or at least to speak out; but he was, by temperament and perhaps also conviction, "one of the venerators," and therefore "not about to set things wrong or right."

Disappointing to the activists, surely; and yet what if the activists' minds had been furnished as Heaney's was? What if they had known in their bones the human cost of pain that cannot be forgotten, pain so disorienting that it deprives the mind of a fair and just assessment of persons and events?

I spoke in the previous chapter of Dorothy Osborne as a great chronicler of the human comedy; Heaney knows its tragedy. He knows it firsthand, as a twentieth-century Irishman; but that is not enough. John Stuart Mill famously wrote about those who would argue for some position in the public arena, "He who knows only his own side of the case knows little of that." We could equally well say that those who know only their own moment in history know little of that—and that they, and their whole culture, are worse for their ignorance. We live thinly in our instant, and don't know what we don't know.

The costs to our personal density are great, but the costs to our descendants may be even greater. Forty years ago, the German philosopher Hans Jonas, in a book that would prove a vital inspiration for the Green movement in his country, asked this potent question: "What force shall represent the future in the present?" What laws and what norms will embody our care for those who come after us, including those already here and those yet to be born? But this is a question that we cannot ask if our thoughts are imprisoned by the stimulation of what rolls across our social media feeds.

Early in this book I quoted a famous line from L. P. Hartley's novel *The Go-Between*: "The past is a foreign country; they do things differently there." Perhaps even more frequently quoted is a sentence by William Faulkner that expresses what looks like the opposite view: "The past is never dead; it's not even past." Both statements are true. The decisions of our ancestors, however strange those people may be to us, touch us and our world; and our decisions will touch the lives of those who come after us. By understanding what moved them and what they hoped for, we give ourselves a better chance of acting wisely—in some cases, as those ancestors *did*; in others, as they *didn't*. We judge them, as we should, as we must; but if we judge them fairly and proportionately, as we ourselves hope someday to be judged, then we may use them well with an eye toward the future. Simone Weil, as we saw, recommends studying the past because the past may sometimes be more than we are, while the future, being imagined by us, is confined by our limitations. But I do not wholly agree: *if* our imaginings of the future are grounded in a deep and sympathetic knowledge of the past, then we may have the personal density required to imagine a future that lies beyond the confines of our experience.

In a 1980 essay, "Standing by Words," the poet and farmer Wendell Berry describes a cultural moment—one of which we are now experiencing in a later and more fully developed stage of it—that militates against accountability for words. One of the manifold ways in which one can fail to be accountable for one's words is to be a *futurist*. Berry shrewdly compares our futurists to the "Projectors" of the Grand Academy of Lagado in Swift's *Gulliver's Travels*: men who appear to be meaningfully related to the future but are in fact wholly self-absorbed. Their future is entirely fictitious, and as Berry says of the Projectors' heirs, our contemporary futurists, their language "drifts inevitably toward the merely provisional. . . . It is not language that the user will very likely be required to stand by or to act on, for it does not define any personal ground for standing or acting. Its only practical utility is to support with 'expert opinion' a vast, impersonal technological action already begun." For Projectors and futurists, "all the grand perfect dreams of the technologists are happening in the future, but nobody is there." Their imagined world is devoid of actual persons, and much of the rest of Creation as well.

But if one is not to be a Projector, what better attitude

might one have toward the future? For Berry, the vital distinction is between *projecting* and *promising*: "The 'projecting' of 'futurologists' uses the future as the safest possible context for whatever is desired; it binds one only to selfish interest. But making a promise binds one to someone else's future." It is this distinction that points us toward the means of fulfilling what Hans Jonas called the "imperative of responsibility." And oddly enough, we begin to make promises to others by having a secure, a substantial, a *dense* place of our own in the world. As Berry says, "We are speaking where we stand, and we shall stand afterwards in the presence of what we have said." Think of Seamus Heaney shin-deep in the waters off Inishowen, standing firmly, against all the vast social and political and technological forces surrounding him, in his "free state of image and allusion."

By taking responsibility for our words—which only those who are anchored, who are minimally vulnerable to "the wind-blown Gods of the Market Place," can do—we step away from the "merely provisional" uses of language and toward genuine accountability. By increasing our personal density we also increase our power to make genuine *promises*—and, as the writer Francis Spufford has said, "You keep the past connected to the present, and to the future, by keeping your promises."* In making those promises, we

---

*He does this in the context of reflecting on the experience he had, as an English child, reading the novels of Laura Ingalls Wilder. "Usually Americans focus on the future, and kick yesterday impatiently out of tomorrow's path. On the prairie, on the other hand, people shrewdly suspected that the past had survival value, and they were, to boot, stubborn. You had to be stubborn to stay. You had to be stubborn to go on making the farmer's bet against drought and deluge every year," Spufford observes in *The Child That Books Built* (London: Faber & Faber, 2002). Which is a useful reminder that no one will do any of the things I counsel in this book without possessing the virtue of stubbornness.

take a step toward giving those who come after us clean earth to till. I am quoting the wizard Gandalf there, who says to his colleagues, "It is not our part to master all the tides of the world, but to do what is in us for the succour of those years wherein we are set, uprooting the evil in the fields that we know, so that those who live after may have clean earth to till. What weather they shall have is not ours to rule." But I am not sure about that second sentence. The weather of the future—and I speak both metaphorically and literally—may also largely depend on the promises we make, and our fidelity in keeping them.

CONCLUSION

———————

One of the most popular novels of the eighteenth century was *Julie, or the New Heloise* by Jean-Jacques Rousseau: an epistolary novel, representing the correspondence of two star-crossed lovers. It can be difficult for today's reader to understand its popularity, because it has a great many passages like this, from a letter written by the book's hero Saint-Preux to his beloved Julie:

> I arrived last evening in Paris, and he who could not live two streets from you is now more than a hundred leagues away. O Julie! pity me, pity your unhappy friend. Had I traced that endless road in long streams of my blood, it would have seemed less long to me, and I would not have felt my soul falter in greater languor. Ah if only I knew the moment that is to reunite us as well as the space that separates us, I would offset the leagues of distance with the progress of time, and in each day subtracted from my life I would count the steps that would have brought me closer to you! But this path of pain is engulfed in the gloom of the future: the end that is to limit it eludes my feeble sight. O doubt! O torture! My anxious heart looks for you and finds nothing. The sun rises and no longer brings me

back the hope of seeing you; it sets and I have not seen you: my days devoid of pleasure and joy flow into a long night. In vain do I wish to rekindle spent hope in me, it offers me but a precarious resource and dubious consolations. Dear and tender friend of my heart, alas! what woes must I anticipate, if they are to equal my earlier happiness?

Six hundred pages of this kind of thing is . . . need I say more? But Robert Darnton, the great historian of eighteenth-century France, thinks that *Julie* was almost certainly *the* best-selling book of its century. Certainly it made Rousseau a literary superstar. He received cartloads of fan letters, many of them in a style quite like the book's: "I dare not tell you the effect it made on me. No, I was past weeping. A sharp pain convulsed me. My heart was crushed." One regular theme of these letters is their writers' belief that the story could not possibly be fictional: "I implore you, Monsieur, tell me: did Julie really live? Is Saint-Preux still alive? What country on this earth does he inhabit? Claire, sweet Claire, did she follow her dear friend to the grave?"

I *could* spend some time here asking an important question: How is it possible that a story that at one time conquered the whole French-speaking world is so inaccessible to us today? All of Rousseau's other major works are widely read, in French and in translation, taught in colleges and universities everywhere, but this one, so obsessively beloved in the author's lifetime, has disappeared from view. How did that happen? It's worth thinking about, because, as I have argued in these pages, what separates us from the past is often just as important as what links us. But for now, as my own little story draws to a close, I want to look at something that we just might connect with: Saint-Preux's entry into Paris. Because he doesn't just miss his beloved Julie, he's very disoriented by life in the big city—an alien place to him, a native of a village in the Alps.

Saint-Preux, in the same letter I quoted from above, insists repeatedly that no pleasure in the city can compare with thoughts of Julie herself: "I spend my entire day in society, I lend my ears and eyes to everything that strikes them, and perceiving nothing that is like you, I collect myself amidst the noise and converse secretly with you"—and yet, day by day, he finds himself drawn more and more into the city's patterns. But he does not know how to interpret them. If he takes the stance of the philosopher, he is too far away from the phenomena he wants to understand; if he plays the role of the "man of the world," that draws him too close.

To recall the R. A. Lafferty story I mentioned early in this book, every night in Paris is, for Saint-Preux, a "Slow Tuesday Night": "since all is but vain appearance and everything changes at every moment, I have no time to be moved by anything, nor to examine anything." But the problem is not only, and not even primarily, one of rushed perception: the "social acceleration" he's experiencing changes him *morally*. He feels that he is "forced to change the order of [his] moral affections, forced to attribute a value to fantasies, and impose silence on nature and reason." The result, he says, is: "I drift from whim to whim, and my tastes being constantly enslaved to opinion, I cannot a single day be sure what I will love the next."

Surely this is just the theme with which we began: the way an environment of high *informational* density produces people of low *personal* density. A world that seems to give us infinite choice actually makes choice nearly impossible: *the informational context chooses for us.* And what that means—Rousseau brings us something new here, something essential—is that our web of information determines what we *love.* Thus Saint-Preux: from day to day, "I cannot be sure what I will love."

To practice positive selection (chapter 3) in relation to the past, to seek the authentic kernel (chapter 5) of human connection, human value—such admirable ideas! Such noble ambitions are contained within them! But ideas and ambitions aren't worth much unless they are transformed into a settled disposition, a habit of mind. And what I'm talking about, and indeed have been talking about throughout this book, is the need for *a disposition to love*: to love the too-often-neglected voices from our past, from the world's past. In chapter 2 I said that "what the dead we encounter in books demand is only the blood of our attention," but we will give even that metaphorical blood only in the cause of love—love of *something*, if only of power. But what I counsel is to give the dead the blood of our attention for our own sake, to enrich and strengthen our identities, to make ourselves more solid and less tenuous—and then, I suggest in chapter 9, to use the solidity we have gained to help us make meaningful promises to the future.

But it's not quite as simple as that. There's an important sense in which we cannot use the past to love ourselves unless we also learn to love our ancestors. We must see them not as *others* but as *neighbors*—and then, ultimately, as kin, as members of our (very) extended family. It is in this cause that throughout this book I have quoted writers who, like C. V. Wedgwood, wish to restore for us the "immediacy of experience" of those who walked this world before us. These are the writers who help us to encounter our ancestors not as anthropological curiosities whom we observe from a critical distance, but as those with whom we can, and should, break bread.

When we own our kinship to those people, they may come alive for us not just as exemplars of narrowness and wickedness that we have overcome, but as neighbors and even as teachers. When we acknowledge that even when they go far astray they do so in ways that we surely would have, had we been formed as they were, we extend them not just attention but love, the very love that we hope our descendants will extend to us. The argument that I have made here for the cultivation of personal density is also an argument for serving as links in the living chain that extends into the distant past and also into the distant future. It is an argument for a genealogy of love.

A Word to the Reader

Throughout these pages I have spoken of "old books," and though there are many other old things worthy of our attention, I chose to focus on the *words* of the past. That wasn't an easy decision for me to make, but I hope it was the right one.

Paul Connerton, in his book *How Modernity Forgets*, describes the ways that places, public and private alike, can be the markers and even the instantiations of memory. A public square named for a hero of the past or a momentous event serves a function similar to the wall of photographs or collection of memorabilia in a "family room"; it is a reminder of inherited identity—which is why after a divorce a painting bought on the honeymoon might be removed to the attic, and why the French Revolutionaries renamed the Pont Notre-Dame the Pont de la Raison.

Architecture speaks, after a fashion, and the old Pont Notre-Dame, with its ramshackle houses perched thereon, did not exactly cry out *La Raison!*—the demolition of those houses a few years before the Revolution may have made the renaming easier. Sometimes the buildings of Paris spoke out more forcefully: one cannot look very closely at the Panthéon without discerning its ecclesiastical origins (it was formerly the Church of St. Genevieve). But such voices are muted in comparison to those of human persons. Photographs, of one's ancestors for instance, are more telling, though they don't literally tell—even the photos in Harry Potter's world, though they move, remain silent. And often photographs, or buildings and their ruins, can speak to us only because of the words that have preceded our encounters with them. Samuel Johnson once wrote, "That man is little to be envied whose patriotism would not gain force upon the plain of Marathon or whose piety would not grow warmer among the ruins of Iona." But what would we know of Marathon without Herodotus, or of Iona without the Venerable Bede?

But what if one's ancestors did speak?

In a lovely and powerful essay, the English writer Paul Kingsnorth describes his experience of visiting the Salon Noir, the Black Chamber in the Niaux Cave in the French Pyrenees.

All around the walls of the Black Chamber are hundreds of line drawings depicting great mammals: herds of bison, pairs of mammoths, groups of ibex. They are painted elegantly, sweepingly, and with clear expertise. Whoever drew these creatures was not doing it for the first time: these were artists who knew their work well. They also knew the animals: the anatomical detail is finely observed, right down to the beards on the ibex and the anal flaps on the mammoths.

But why are the paintings there? Kingsnorth points out that, though people speak of "hunting scenes," none of the animals are being hunted, and indeed paleoanthropologists believe that the people who painted those creatures—they are called Magdalenians—did not eat them: analysis of their bones suggests that they ate reindeer, but there are no reindeer on the walls of the Black Chamber. So, the question returns: Why did these people, some fifteen thousand years ago, paint animals, and paint them with such (apparently) loving attention? And that question leads Kingsnorth to larger ones: "What was the world, to them, and what spirits haunted it? What stories did they tell about their place here, about the past and present? Who, what, did they think they were?"

Kingsnorth understands how limited our knowledge of the Magdalenians is, how little we know of their lives, much less their thoughts. But he hazards a guess—or rather, experiences an intuition:

> It seems obvious to me—and I think the scant evidence bears it out—that whatever happened in the Black Chamber was not driven by utility. Whoever was here, and whatever they were doing, they were forging a connection to something way beyond everyday reality. These paintings are not expressions of economics or natural history. They surely sprang from the same sense of power and smallness and wonder and awe that I feel as I stand in the same place that the artists would have stood. This was a reaching out to, for, something way beyond human comprehension. This was a meeting with the sacred.

Kingsnorth may be right about this—I freely admit that I want him to be right—but we do not know and will never know. Nothing we could ever learn about these preliterate people will answer the kinds of questions Kingsnorth asks. The paintings in the Black Chamber are eloquent, but in a peculiar way: it is an eloquence that hides as much as it reveals.

Hugh Kenner makes the shrewd comment that after 1870 or so it became possible, thanks to the findings of archaeologists and their transfer to what are now the great European museums, for many people to see artifacts from the distant past and hold them in their own hands—and he then goes on to discuss the cave art itself: "The shock lay in this, that the horses and deer and aurochs brought the eye such immediacy of perception, though a disregard of up and down and through made them inconceivable in to-day's canons: and yet they seemed not to rely on yesterday's canons either. They simply existed outside of history. . . . Time folded over; now lay flat, transparent, upon not-now." And what lives outside of history cannot speak to us clearly. If it is not utterly mute, at best it mumbles, and we struggle to sort out the possible meanings.

Such ambiguity is intrinsic to the physical remains of our past. Some years ago, when I visited Rome for the first time and was wandering through the Forum, I kept noticing, as I tried to compose artful photographs, the proud bulk of the Victor Emmanuel Monument, the Altare della Patria, looming above every object in the Forum. I found this unwanted presence extremely annoying: the building seemed to me so tasteless, so bombastic, so obviously jeal-

ous of the beauties of Ancient Rome, so shamelessly determined to exceed them. It was, I thought, a monument to
hubris.

Somewhat later, I did some reading and learned that my
instinctive reaction was, if not necessarily altogether wrong,
certainly incomplete, inadequate. The building of the Altare della Patria was a key component of the Risorgimento,
the renewal of Italian culture and polity, the hoped-for
shaping of a fragmented peninsula into a modern nation-
state. It sought to honor the Roman past as much as to compete with it. What I was sure I heard the monument saying
was at best a fragment, or a distortion. And that was perhaps inevitable, because I was trying to translate into words
something whose native language was not words but rather
mass, shape, form—designed and built materials, deployed
in space.

To see the art of our ancestors can be an incredibly powerful thing; but we want also, we can't help but want also,
the human voice, to hear those who came before us speak
to us. And when they do speak with a human tongue, even
when it's in writing, they make themselves hard to ignore.
The Israeli historian Yuval Noah Harari has spoken of the
revelation that came to him when he realized that Jerusalem
is "just stones." Just stones! Well, one can choose to see
them that way. But no one can pick up an old book, open it,
and think: just marks. Just ink sprayed on wood pulp. We
may despise the words written there, or think them irrelevant, but we can't escape knowing what they are. Another
human being from another world has spoken to us.

In the mid-1950s, when Robert Moses was the most

powerful man in New York City, he oversaw the construction of a convention center at Columbus Circle that he called, and caused others to call, the New York Coliseum. Years later, when Robert Caro was writing his biography of Moses, Moses cooperated, but would regularly ask of the book, scornfully, "How long will it last? In a short while, it will be yesterday's news"—not worthy to be compared to a mighty coliseum.

Late in the year 1999, Caro watched from the window of his office as workers began dismantling the Coliseum, which has since been replaced by the Time Warner Center. Relating this story to a journalist, Caro said, "When they tore it down, I felt something about books."

Envoi

Farewell, little book: go forth into the world and, if you can, do some good. I at least will always be in your debt. You gave me many sweet months when, as people told me breathlessly of the latest astonishing video or the latest appalling tweet, I could say, *I'm sorry, I know nothing about all that, for I have been thinking of old books, and to that work I must return.*

Acknowledgments

My thanks go first of all to the critical eye and generous spirit of my editor, Ginny Smith; to Caroline Sydney and the other excellent staff at Penguin Press, including the attentive editors-of-copy; and to my extraordinary agent, Christy Fletcher, for bringing all of us together.

I also am grateful for friends who gave me encouragement and constructive criticism, in various proportions, along the way: Garnette Cadogan, Elizabeth Corey, Beverly Gaventa, Richard Gibson, Wesley Hill, James Davison Hunter, Tim Larsen, Edward Mendelson, Rob Miner, Adam Roberts, Dan Treier—and especially Francis Spufford, who gave wise counsel at a key moment. My warmest thanks to Amana Fontanella-Khan of *The Guardian* of London for commissioning, editing, and running the essay that became the trial balloon for this book. I ask forgiveness from those whose aid I have forgotten.

In the time of writing, my wife, Teri, and my son, Wesley, have, in the various ways to which they are accustomed, kept me sane and grounded and, at least occasionally, humble.

I have dedicated this book to the memory of my dear

friend Brett Foster, who took the greatest delight in breaking bread with the dead. His copy of David Ferry's translation of Horace's *Odes*, bedecked with sticky notes covered
in spidery handwriting, stuffed with photocopied poems,
annotated with a blizzard of tiny pencil marks, was by my
side as I wrote this book. *Caro amico*, how I miss you.

Notes

Introduction

1 **"a tranquil mind":** Horace, *The Epistles of Horace: Bilingual Edition*, trans. David Ferry (New York: Macmillan, 2002), I.18.

2 **"like a psychopath":** Jason Gay, tweet of September 22, 2015, https://twitter .com/jasongay/status/646301750346010624.

5 **"pressure for foresight":** Norbert Elias, *The Civilizing Process: Sociogenetic and Psychogenetic Investigations*, trans. Edmund Jephcott (New York: Wiley, 2000), part 4, ch. 2.

5 **young people today:** See, for instance, recent reflections by Tess Brigham (https://www.cnbc.com/2019/07/02/a-millennial-therapist-brings-up-the -biggest-complaint-they-bring-up-in-therapy.html) and Loren Soeiro (https:// www.psychologytoday.com/us/blog/i-hear-you/201907/why-are-millennials -so-anxious-and-unhappy).

6 **"The past is a foreign country":** L. P. Hartley, *The Go-Between* (1953; repr., New York: NYRB Classics, 2002), 16.

7 **absence of climate change:** Amitav Ghosh, *The Great Derangement: Climate Change and the Unthinkable* (Chicago: University of Chicago Press, 2016). The interview with Wen Stephenson appeared in *The Baffler* (https://thebaffler .com/latest/divining-comedy-stephenson). The novel in which Ghosh draws on what he learned from pre-modern Bengali literature is *Gun Island* (New York: Farrar, Straus & Giroux, 2019).

1: Presentism and Temporal Bandwidth

11 **racist, sexist colonialism:** Charles Boyle's denunciation of Robinson Crusoe is in *The Guardian*: https://www.theguardian.com/books/2019/apr/19/robin son-crusoe-at-300-its-time-to-let-go-of-this-toxic-colonial-fairytale.

11 **a librarian grieves:** Sofia Leung on library collections proliferating white-ness: https://sleung.wordpress.com/2019/04/15/whiteness-as-collections/.

12 **the burning of Notre-Dame:** Patricio del Real of Harvard is quoted saying of Notre-Dame that "the building was so overburdened with meaning that its

burning feels like an act of liberation" at https://www.rollingstone.com/culture /culture-features/notre-dame-cathedral-paris-fire-whats-next-822743/.

12 **This business of defilement:** I explain more thoroughly what I mean by "defilement" in "Wokeness and Myth on Campus," *The New Atlantis*, Summer /Fall 2017.

12 *social acceleration:* Hartmut Rosa, *Social Acceleration: A New Theory of Modernity*, trans. Jonathan Trejo-Mathys (New York: Columbia University Press, 2013). This magnificent book is too technical for me to share in undiluted form, but it has been essential to my thinking about my whole project. My debt to Rosa is immense.

13 **"attentional commons":** Matthew Crawford, "The Costs of Paying Attention," *The New York Times*, March 7, 2015.

13 **"Ildefonsa Impala":** Lafferty's books go in and out of print, but "Slow Tuesday Night" may be found in a collection called *Nine Hundred Grandmothers* (New York: Ace, 1970). The collection has been reprinted several times by other publishers.

15 **"Speed is the god":** Stefan Breuer, quoted in Rosa, *Social Acceleration*, 14.

15 **"end of history":** Fukuyama, *The End of History and the Last Man* (New York: Penguin, 1993), 66.

15 **"frenetic standstill":** The phrase, which Rosa quotes often, comes originally from Paul Virilio. It's the English translation of Rosa's German version (*rasender Stillstand*) of Virilio's *L'Inertie polaire* (the title of a book he published in French in 1990, which later was translated into English as *Polar Inertia*). "Frenetic standstill" is an excellent phrase.

16 **"the reason so many":** Clay Routledge, "From Academia to Hollywood: An Interview with Tony Tost," *Quillette*, July 13, 2019, https://quillette.com/2019 /07/13/academia-and-hollywood-an-interview-with-tony-tost/.

17 **"the baby, assailed":** William James, *The Principles of Psychology* (New York: Henry Holt, 1890), ch. 17, "Sensation."

18 **"liquidating a people":** Milan Kundera, *The Book of Laughter and Forgetting*, trans. Aaron Asher (New York: HarperPerennial, 1994), 218.

18 **"For the principle":** Thomas Hobbes's remarks are in "To the Readers," in his translation of Thucydides's *The Peloponnesian War* (1628; repr., Chicago: University of Chicago Press, 2008), xxi.

19 **"Personal density":** Thomas Pynchon, *Gravity's Rainbow* (1973; repr., New York: Penguin, 2012), 509.

20 **"You must change your life":** "Archaic Torso of Apollo," in *The Selected Poetry of Rainer Maria Rilke*, trans. Stephen Mitchell (1982; repr., New York: Vintage, 1989), 61.

20 **"conduct of life":** Gerd-Günter Voss is quoted in Rosa, *Social Acceleration*, 236–37.

22 **"wind-borne Gods":** Kipling's poem "The Gods of the Copybook Headings," which we shall return to later, is widely available online.

23 **"Older and adult art":** Routledge, "From Academia to Hollywood."

24 **"Some things benefit from shocks":** Nassim Nicholas Taleb, *Antifragile: Things That Gain from Disorder* (New York: Random House, 2012), 4.

25 **"it is a crucial fact":** Charles Taylor, *A Secular Age* (Cambridge: The Belknap Press of Harvard University Press, 2007), 28–29.

25 **"escape the gnarled hands":** Christopher Hitchens, *God Is Not Great: How Religion Poisons Everything* (New York: Twelve, 2007), 283.

2: Table Fellowship

27 **"Art is our chief means":** This is an image that Auden seems to have come up with late in his life, but he liked it enough to use it repeatedly. Its first occurrence, I believe, came in a lecture he delivered in 1967: "Let us remember that though the great artists of the past could not change the course of history, it is only through their work that we are able to break bread with the dead, and without communion with the dead a fully human life is impossible." W. H. Auden, *The Complete Works of W. H. Auden*, vol. 5, *Prose: 1963–1968*, ed. Edward Mendelson (Princeton, N.J.: Princeton University Press, 2015), 477.

28 **"because they live impurely":** A readily accessible source for the Clementine Homilies is http://www.newadvent.org/fathers/0808.htm. Homily 13 is the one I have quoted.

30 **"there is a case":** David Cannadine, *The Undivided Past: Humanity Beyond Our Differences* (New York: Knopf, 2013), 5–6.

31 **"I note the obvious differences":** Maya Angelou, *I Shall Not Be Moved: Poems* (New York: Random House, 2011), 5.

31 **"staying with the trouble":** Donna Haraway, *Staying with the Trouble: Making Kin in the Chthulucene* (Durham, N.C.: Duke University Press, 2016), 3, 209.

32 **a tripartite distinction:** Scott Alexander's ingroup/outgroup/fargroup tripod is developed in a 2014 post called "I Can Tolerate Anything except the Outgroup," https://slatestarcodex.com/2014/09/30/i-can-tolerate-anything -except-the-outgroup/.

33 **"I don't want anyone":** Brian Morton, "Virginia Woolf? Snob! Richard Wright? Sexist! Dostoyevsky? Anti-Semite!," *The New York Times*, January 8, 2019, https://www.nytimes.com/2019/01/08/books/review/edith-wharton -house-of-mirth-anti-semitism.html.

35 **"If a lion could speak":** Ludwig Wittgenstein, *Philosophical Investigations*, ed. P. M. S. Hacker and Joachim Schulte, 4th ed. (Oxford: Blackwell, 2009), 223.

35 **"What Is It Like":** Thomas Nagel, "What Is It Like to Be a Bat?," *Philosophical Review* 83, no. 4 (October 1974): 435–50.

35 **"In hunting with Mabel":** Helen Macdonald, *H Is for Hawk* (New York: Grove Atlantic, 2014), 210.

36 **"the past offers us":** Simone Weil, "The Romanesque Renaissance," in *Selected Essays, 1934–1943: Historical, Political, and Moral Writings*, trans. Richard Rees (Eugene, Ore.: Wipf & Stock, 2015), 44.

38 **"Now I am going":** Quoted in Anita Desai, *Clear Light of Day* (London: Penguin, 1980), 167, 174.

40 **"The Long Now Foundation hopes":** http://longnow.org/about/.

40 **"If we want":** Brian Eno, "The Big Here and Long Now": http://longnow.org /essays/big-here-and-long-now/.

42 **"For those dreamers"**: Weil, "The *Iliad*, or the Poem of Force," trans. Mary McCarthy, *Chicago Review* 18, no. 2 (1965): 5–30.

3: The Sins of the Past

46 **"Admiring the great thinkers"**: Julian Baggini, "Why Sexist and Racist Philosophers Might Still Be Admirable," *Aeon*, https://aeon.co/ideas/why-sexist-and -racist-philosophers-might-still-be-admirable.

48 **"Whether we should kill"**: Thomas Nagel, "What We Owe a Rabbit," *New York Review of Books*, March 21, 2019, https://www.nybooks.com/articles/2019 /03/21/christine-korsgaard-what-we-owe-a-rabbit/.

49 **"It seems almost incredible"**: John Dewey, *Democracy and Education: An Introduction to the Philosophy of Education* (New York: Macmillan, 1916), 20.

49 extremely useful distinction: Alyssa Vance, "Positive and Negative Selection," *The Rationalist Conspiracy* (blog), June 19, 2012, https://rationalconspir acy.com/2012/06/19/negative-and-positive-selection/. Scott Alexander's use of Vance's idea is at https://slatestarcodex.com/2019/02/26/rule-genius-in-not -out/. He concludes his post thus: "Some of the people who have most inspired me have been inexcusably wrong on basic issues. But you only need one world-changing revelation to be worth reading."

52 **"books freely permitted"**: John Milton's *Areopagitica* is widely available online, for instance in this well-prepared version: https://www.dartmouth.edu /~milton/reading_room/areopagitica/text.html.

55 **"The highest ideals"**: C. V. Wedgwood, *The King's Peace: 1637–1641* (1955; repr., New York: Book of the Month Club, 1991), 16.

56 **"visited rustic and neglected"**: Claude Lévi-Strauss, *Tristes Tropiques*, trans. John Weightman and Doreen Weightman (1955; repr., London: Penguin, 2012), 384.

4: The Past Without Difference

61 **"until the 18th Cent."**: I quote this letter in my introduction to the critical edition of Auden's 1944 poem *For the Time Being: A Christmas Oratorio* (Princeton, N.J.: Princeton University Press, 2013), xxi.

62 **"it was a common romantic vice"**: C. V. Wedgwood, *The Sense of the Past* (Cambridge: Cambridge University Press, 1957), 6.

63 **"When evening has come"**: J. R. Hale, ed., *The Literary Works of Machiavelli* (Oxford: Oxford University Press, 1961), 372.

66 **"Although I originally took"**: Plutarch, *Roman Lives*, trans. Robin Waterfield (New York: Oxford University Press, 1999), 42.

67 The king asked West: Garry Wills, *Cincinnatus: George Washington and the Enlightenment* (New York: Doubleday, 1984), 13.

69 **"Someone—I forget who"**: Quoted in Andrew Roberts, *Churchill: Walking with Destiny* (London: Penguin, 2018), 116.

69 **"the mind of man"**: Chesterton's essay "On Man: Heir of All the Ages" may be found in many places online, for instance, http://www.gkc.org.uk/gkc/books /Avowals_and_Denials.html#13.

71 **"peace it bodes":** *The Taming of the Shrew*, V.ii.

71 **"are very startling to":** C. S. Lewis, *A Preface to Paradise Lost* (London: Oxford University Press, 1942), 76.

72 **"In a classic we":** Italo Calvino, "Why Read the Classics?," *New York Review of Books*, October 9, 1986, https://www.nybooks.com/articles/1986/10/09/why-read-the-classics/.

73 **"Opposition is true friendship":** The sentence is found in some, but not all, copies of Blake's *The Marriage of Heaven and Hell* (1793); see, for instance, the edition with commentary by Geoffrey Keynes (Oxford: Oxford University Press, 1975), xxv.

74 **"generations of emperors and generals":** Daniel Mendelsohn, "Is the *Aeneid* a Celebration of Empire—or a Critique?," *The New Yorker*, October 15, 2018, https://www.newyorker.com/magazine/2018/10/15/is-the-aeneid-a-celebration-of-empire-or-a-critique.

75 **"very queer book":** Philip Hoare, "Subversive, Queer and Terrifyingly Relevant: Six Reasons Why *Moby-Dick* Is the Novel for Our Times," *The Guardian*, July 30, 2019, https://www.theguardian.com/books/2019/jul/30/subversive-queer-and-terrifyingly-relevant-six-reasons-why-moby-dick-is-the-novel-for-our-times.

76 **"aged seventy-seven":** Tom Stoppard, *The Invention of Love* (New York: Grove Press, 1998), 1.

78 **"We thus reach":** Dewey, *Democracy and Education*, 89.

79 **"The lyf so short":** The first line of Chaucer's *Parlement of Foules* (Parliament of Birds).

79 **"What we have loved":** The line may be found near the very end of the fourteenth book of Wordsworth's long poem *The Prelude* (widely available online)—at least in the 1850 edition. Rather than "we will teach them how," the 1805 edition had the more modest "we *may* teach them how." Perhaps the poet grew more confident with age.

5: The Authentic Kernel

81 **honestly and intelligently:** Patrocinio Schweickart's essay has been extremely widely anthologized, for instance in *Feminisms: An Anthology of Literary Theory and Criticism*, ed. Robyn R. Warhol, and Diane Price Herndl (New Brunswick, N.J.: Rutgers University Press, 1997), 609–34.

84 **"No doubt I will":** Ursula K. Le Guin, *Lavinia* (New York: Mariner Books, 2009), 4.

86 **"generosity as an enduring habit":** Kathleen Fitzpatrick, *Generous Thinking: A Radical Approach to Saving the University* (Baltimore: Johns Hopkins University Press, 2019), 56. Fitzpatrick is very shrewd on the ways that the academic profession—and this is true of many other professions—pays lip service to generosity but also builds up a structure of incentives that actively resists generosity: "This mode of generous thinking is thus first and foremost a willingness to think *with* someone. Scholars frequently engage in this kind of work with close colleagues, in various ways—when we read their in-preparation manuscripts in order

to help improve them, for instance—but it's an orientation to scholarly conversation that rapidly diminishes as we move outside our immediate circles and turn to the more public performance of our academic selves. In those modes of interaction we often feel ourselves required to become more critical—or more competitive—and we frequently find ourselves focusing not on the substance of what is being said to us, but on the gaps or missteps that give us openings to defend our own positions. . . . [Note how this tendency promotes negative rather than positive selection.] As a result, while we may understand generosity of mind to be a key value within the profession, its actual enactment is not allowed to become habitual, not encouraged to become part of our general mode of being" (55).

6: The Boy in the Library

92 **"the impact of a revelation":** Peter Abrahams's autobiography, *Tell Freedom* (London: Faber & Faber, 1954), is an absolute masterpiece, and I consider it something close to tragedy that it has so often been out of print in the United States. The key passages I draw on are from 187–89 (the street-corner meeting), 192–93 (reading Du Bois), and 199–200 (the decision to go to England).

93 **"I was fourteen":** Zadie Smith, "That Crafty Feeling," in *Changing My Mind: Occasional Essays* (New York: Penguin Press, 2009), 103.

96 **"I was now about twelve":** From *The Narrative of the Life of Frederick Douglass, in The Portable Frederick Douglass*, ed. John Stauffer and Henry Louis Gates Jr. (New York: Penguin, 2016), 180.

97 **"I was treacherously kidnapped":** I have used the 1816 edition of *The Columbian Orator*, which can be found on Google Books: https://books.google.com/books?id=c58AAAAAYAAJ (240).

101 **essayist Leslie Jamison:** Rachel Toliver, "A Conversation with Leslie Jamison," *Image*, issue 101, https://imagejournal.org/article/leslie-jamison/.

7: The Stoics' Moment

104 **"Only Epictetus understood":** Tom Wolfe, *A Man in Full* (New York: Farrar, Straus & Giroux, 1998), 411, 443.

106 **"Many men are attracted":** Donna Zuckerberg, *Not All Dead White Men: Classics and Misogyny in the Digital Age* (Cambridge, Mass.: Harvard University Press, 2018), 59.

108 **The manosphere is repeatedly shown:** An interesting recent paper attempts to quantify the misogyny of the manosphere and demonstrates that the climate there is just as bad as Zukerberg suggests. See Tracie Farrell, Miriam Fernandez, Jakub Novotny, and Harith Alani, "Exploring Misogyny across the Manosphere in Reddit," in *WebSci '19: Proceedings of the 10th ACM Conference on Web Science* (2019), 87–96, http://oro.open.ac.uk/61128/.

109 **"By analyzing and deconstructing":** Zuckerberg, *Not All Dead White Men*, 9, 49.

109 **"a rational, science-friendly philosophy":** Massimo Pigliucci, *How to Be a Stoic: Using Ancient Philosophy to Live a Modern Life* (New York: Basic Books, 2017), 5.

110 **"Pigliucci contends":** Carlos Fraenkel, "Can Stoicism Make Us Happy?," *The Nation*, February 5, 2019, https://www.thenation.com/article/massimo -pigliucci-modern-stoicism-book-review/.

111 **"when approaching the past":** Mark Lilla, "My Totally Correct Views on Everything," Tocqueville21, September 4, 2018, https://tocqueville21.com /focus/my-totally-correct-views-on-everything/.

111 **"This book is not":** C. V. Wedgwood, *The King's Peace* (1955; repr. New York: Book of the Month Club, 1991), 17.

113 **"I happen to believe":** Brian Phillips, "The Magical Thinking of the Far Right," *The Ringer*, December 12, 2018, https://www.theringer.com/2018/12/12 /18137221/far-right-occult-symbols.

114 **"The varieties of false knowledge":** Terry Teachout's review of Lucas Hnath's *A Doll's House, Part 2*—about which more later—appeared in *The Wall Street Journal* on April 27, 2017, https://www.wsj.com/articles/a-dolls-house -part-2-review-an-unneeded-sequel-1493339401, under the title "'A Doll's House, Part 2' Review: An Unneeded Sequel."

114 **"to honor their memory":** The speech appears in *The Portable Frederick Douglass* (195–222) under the title "What to the Slave Is the Fourth of July?"

8: The View from the Doll's House

121 **"Mr. Courtenay expresses":** Thomas Babington Macaulay's review may be found online at https://oll.libertyfund.org/titles/macaulay-critical-and -historical-essays-vol-3/simple.

122 **"that religion or honor":** There is, to the eternal shame of the publishing industry, no truly readable edition of Osborne's letters, but you may find a decent version online at http://digital.library.upenn.edu/women/osborne /letters/letters.html.

128 **"pronounced a death sentence":** Quoted in Michael Meyer, *Ibsen* (1967; repr., Harmondsworth, U.K.: Penguin, 1985), which contains an excellent account of the fortunes of the play on 476–81.

130 **"You think no one":** Lucas Hnath, *A Doll's House, Part 2* (New York: Theatre Communications Group, 2018), 95. In quoting from Hnath I have adjusted his eccentric punctuation, which is better suited to actors than to readers.

132 **"The hallmark of":** D. T. Max, "Lucas Hnath Lets Actors Fight It Out Onstage," *The New Yorker*, April 15, 2019, https://www.newyorker.com /magazine/2019/04/22/lucas-hnath-lets-actors-fight-it-out-onstage.

133 **"I can finally see":** Helen Lewis's comments, from the June 19, 2019, issue of the New Statesman, may be found at https://www.newstatesman.com/politics /uk/2019/06/first-thoughts-throbbing-machismo-brexiteers-rise-woke-right -and-farewell-ns.

134 *This American Life:* A transcript of the episode may be found at https://www .thisamericanlife.org/680/transcript.

137 **"Do not chiefly":** Alfred North Whitehead, *Science and the Modern World* (1925; repr., New York: Free Press, 1967), 148.

9: The Poet on the Strand

139 **"wading a shingle beach":** Seamus Heaney, "Sandstone Keepsake," in *Opened Ground: Selected Poems 1966–1996* (New York: Farrar, Straus & Giroux, 1998), 204.

141 **"He pointed out":** Dante, *Inferno* XII.

142 **"He who knows":** John Stuart Mill, *On Liberty* (1860), chapter 2.

143 **"What force shall represent":** Hans Jonas, *The Imperative of Responsibility: In Search of an Ethics for the Technological Age*, trans. Hans Jonas and David Kerr (Chicago: University of Chicago Press, 1985), 1–2.

143 **"The past is never dead":** Words spoken not directly by Faulkner but by one of his recurrent characters, the lawyer Gavin Stevens, in *Requiem for a Nun* (1950; repr., New York: Vintage International, 2011), 74.

144 **"Standing by Words":** This is the title essay of Berry's *Standing by Words* (San Francisco: North Point Press, 1982); see especially 58–62. I have adapted these two paragraphs on Berry from my essay "Tending the Digital Commons: A Small Ethics Toward the Future," *The Hedgehog Review* 20, no. 1 (Spring 2018), 54–66.

146 **"It is not our part":** J. R. R. Tolkien, *The Lord of the Rings: The Return of the King*, 50th Anniversary Edition (Boston: Houghton Mifflin, 2005), 879.

Conclusion

147 **"I arrived last evening":** Jean Jacques Rousseau, *Julie, or the New Heloise: Letters of Two Lovers Who Live in a Small Town at the Foot of the Alps* (Hanover, N.H.: Dartmouth College Press, 1997), book 2, letter 13.

148 **"I dare not tell you":** Robert Darnton records these and other enthusiastic comments in "Readers Respond to Rousseau: The Fabrication of Romantic Sensitivity," chapter 6 of *The Great Cat Massacre and Other Episodes in French Cultural History* (New York: Basic Books, 1984), 215–56.

A Word to the Reader

153 **places, public and private:** Paul Connerton, *How Modernity Forgets* (Cambridge: Cambridge University Press, 2009), 11.

154 **"That man is little":** See the chapter on Inch Kenneth in Samuel Johnson, *A Journey to the Western Isles of Scotland* (1775).

154 **"All around the walls":** Paul Kingsnorth, "In the Black Chamber," in *Confessions of a Recovering Environmentalist and Other Essays* (Minneapolis: Graywolf, 2017), 153–56.

156 **"The shock lay":** Hugh Kenner, *The Mechanic Muse* (Oxford: Oxford University Press, 1987), 30.

157 **"just stones":** Yuval Noah Harari made this comment in conversation with Derek Thompson: https://www.theatlantic.com/business/archive/2017/02/the-post-human-world/517206/.

158 **"How long will it last":** Robert Caro repeated this comment in his 2012 interview with Chris Jones of *Esquire*: https://www.esquire.com/entertainment/books/a13522/robert-caro-0512/. I'm grateful to my editor, Ginny Smith, for calling my attention to it.

Index